AMBASSADOR

BELFAST, NORTHERN IRELAND
GREENVILLE, SOUTH CAROLINA

ISRAEL
AND THE
BLESSING
OF THE
TRIBES

ISRAEL
AND THE
BLESSING
OF THE
TRIBES

E. Bendor Samuel

Israel and the Blessing of the Tribes

This edition 2002

ISBN 1 84030 117 1

Ambassador Books
an imprint of
Ambassador Productions Ltd.
Providence House
Ardenlee Street
Belfast
BT6 8QJ
Northern Ireland
www.ambassador-productions.com

Emerald House Group Inc.
427 Wade Hampton Blvd.
Greenville
SC 29609, USA
www.emeraldhouse.com

Preface

ONCE again we respond to the request of our friends, and publish in book form the leading articles on "The Blessing of the Tribes" that have appeared in our Quarterly, *The Scattered Nation.*

We have, however, re-written it to a great extent, and have considerably enlarged it. All the translations are from the original. We sincerely trust that, true to its name, the book will be made a blessing to many.

These prophecies, both by Jacob, in Genesis 49, and by Moses in Deuteronomy 33, are very important inasmuch they form an introduction to Israel's history, which occupies so much of the Old Testament Scripture. These two chapters give us, indeed, a brief outline, prophetically, of God's dealings with His people, and they contain many lessons for us all of warning and encouragement, exhibiting God's holiness and compassion.

The author is old-fashioned enough to believe that Genesis and Deuteronomy were written by Moses, who was divinely inspired to do so, and that these books are true and reliable records of what they purport to be. and are, therefore, absolutely authoritative and of spiritual significance.

E. BENDOR SAMUEL.

"DORELI,"
    1 LYNFORD GARDENS,
        GOODMAYES, ESSEX.

Contents

THE
BLESSING OF THE TRIBES

CHAPTER I

Introduction

WHAT helpful instruction the Lord has been pleased to give us in the record of His dealings with the ancient patriarchs! Truly, the whole history of Israel, as we have it in the Scriptures, is meant for our learning and profit.

God's Searching Rays of Light.

Exposed to the light of God as no other nation has ever been, their every blemish is illumined and made conspicuous to the gaze of the world. Their sins and shortcomings, their triumphs and achievements are all accurately recorded that we may be warned by their failures and encouraged by their successes.

"All Scripture is given by inspiration of God," says the apostle, "and is profitable for doctrine, for reproof, for correction, for instruction in righteousness: that the man of God may be perfect, throughly furnished unto all good works" (2 Tim. 3. 16, 17).

In the Bible we get an accurate delineation of men's characters; the blemishes of its heroes are given as well as their commendable qualities. It shows us goodness and its reward, also evil and its effect. Frequently the characteristics of the parent re-appear in his descendants. This was the case with some of the tribes of Israel. Everywhere, however, God's controlling hand is clearly manifest.

God's Overruling Grace.

It is striking that six of the tribes descended from the sons of Leah, not from the sons of the beloved Rachel, for whom Jacob was content to labour many years; so that the deception practised on him by Laban, when he gave him Leah to wife instead of Rachel, was overruled for the building up of the Israel nation.

How often the thing that we like least is made to turn out for our highest good! We need grace to take our disappointments as His appointments, for a blessing may be in them.

Jacob's prophecy concerning his sons was in harmony with their character, though in some cases God in His grace overruled the ordinary circumstances in their favour, as in the case of Levi. The door of mercy is left open for the penitent, and where sin abounds grace does much more abound.

The Patriarch's Strong Faith.

The predictions exhibit a strong confidence in God; though uttered in Egypt, when no human sagacity could have foretold future events that would happen in Palestine, they were seen afar off by the patriarchs, who were persuaded of them and embraced them while they were strangers and pilgrims on the earth (Hebrews 11. 13).

We are told that when a man faces death his whole life passes rapidly before his mind. Jacob on his deathbed recalled the important events of his long life, the many vicissitudes through which God so wonderfully led him. This he often recognised (see Gen. 31. 11-13; 35. 2, 3; 48. 15, 16). He speaks of Him as the God that fed, or that shepherded him all his life long—the Angel that redeemed him from all evil. The God of Bethel and the Man of Peniel he here identified with the Angel that redeemed him.

The Lord's gracious dealings with him in the past encouraged him to believe His precious promises for the future. In the blessings he mingled promise and prediction. He himself was about to pass from these earthly scenes, but the Eternal and unchanging God will remain for ever to fulfil His covenant with the generations to come. The divine providence, nay, the Divine Person, that watched over him, protected and guided him (Gen. 28. 13-15; 31. 42) will also protect and guide his sons throughout their national destiny.

The Prediction of Moses.

The Blessing of Moses commences also with a retrospect of the great events in his career, when God personally descended to Mount Sinai—illuminating with His divine light and glory the land of Seir and the mountains of Paran, just as the sun in setting and rising lights up and gilds the floating vapour in the sky (Exod. 19. 16; 20. 18).

The thunder and lightning and flashes of fire accompanying God's presence on Sinai were emblematic of the fiery Law He came to give. It was an exhibition of His own majesty, and at the same time of His great love for Israel, whom He was bringing into covenant relationship with Himself.

All this Moses expressed in his introduction to his blessing of the tribes:

"And this is the blessing wherewith Moses, the man of God, blessed the children of Israel before his death,
And he said,

> Jehovah came from Sinai,
> And rose (as light) from Seir unto them ;
> He shined forth from Mount Paran,
> And He came from ten thousands of holy ones ;
> At His right hand was a fiery law for them.
> Yea, He loveth the people ;
> All His saints are in Thy hand ;
> And they lay down at Thy feet ;
> Every one shall receive of Thy words."
>
> (Deut. 33. 1-3).

Moses saw in God's wonderful descent on Sinai, not only a display of His greatness, but also of His goodness: "He loved the people." This love was the cause and basis of the blessings He bestowed upon them. Our love to Him has its origin in His love to us. "We love Him," says the apostle, "because He first loved us."

> We are on His heart to be loved,
> In His hand to be used,
> At His feet to be taught.

Israel

" I WALKED among the pyramids
  When they were young,
And heard God's living oracles
  Ere Homer sung.

I witnessed Nineveh's dire fall,
  Spite of her might,
And haughty Babylon go down
  In blackest night.

The martial pride of Rome I knew,
  Would have its day ;
I saw her spread like green bay tree,
  Then pass away.

Armies of heathen rushed on me,
  Again, again—
Like monsters to devour me whole—
  Their wrath was vain.

I passed through fire and through flood,
  Yet I am sure,
Mountains may crumble into dust,
  I shall endure.

My name is on Jehovah's hands,
  And on His heart ;
Let hatred do its worst to tear
  My life apart.

Yet for awhile I needs must feel
  The chast'ning rod,
For I have sinned, and I have been
  At odds with God.

The centuries adown I spurned
  Him Whom alone
Heaven found worthy to be placed
  Upon its throne.

But though I still drain sorrow's cup,
  It can't be long,
And He will come and turn my sighs
  To gladsome song.

The clouds are dark, but they are pierced
  By glory bright ;
'Tis written that " at eventide
  It shall be light ! "   MAX. I. REICH.

CHAPTER II

Reuben—The First-born

" And Jacob called unto his sons and said :
Gather yourselves together that I may tell you that
  which shall befall you in the latter days.
Assemble yourselves, and hear, ye sons of Jacob,
And hearken unto Israel your father.
Reuben, thou art my firstborn,
My might and the beginning of my strength ; pre-
  eminent in dignity and pre-eminent in power.
Unstable as water thou shalt not have the pre-
  eminence ;
Because thou wentest up to thy father's bed ;
Then defiledst thou it (he went up to my couch) "
(Gen. 49. 1-4).

" And this is the blessing, wherewith Moses the man
  of God blessed the children of Israel before his
  death.
And he said, . . . ' Let Reuben live, and not die ;
Nor let his men be few ' " (Deut. 33. 1, 6).

CHAPTER II

Reuben—The First-born
(GEN. 49.   DEUT. 33).

THE divine record of Moses is that at the end of his earthly career, when 120 years old, "his eye was not dim, nor his natural force abated" (Deut. 34. 7).   But God's dealing is not the same with all His servants.   We are told that "the eyes of Israel were dim with age so that he could not see" (Gen. 48. 10).

Jacob's Prophetic Vision.

On his death-bed, when his sons were gathered around him to receive his last blessing, he could not see them.   God, however, gave him a vision not only of his own days, but also of the distant history of their descendants to the end of time.   "And Jacob called unto his sons, and said, Gather yourselves together, that I may tell you that which shall befall you in the last days."

This great prophecy is the key to the Scripture narration of Israel's tribes, with whose history the whole Bible is occupied, and who eventually find a place in the restored land of promise (Ezek. 48). Their names are also inscribed on the twelve pearly gates of the heavenly Jerusalem (Rev. 21. 12).   Truly, "the gifts and calling of God are without repentance" (Rom. 11. 29).

On a former occasion Jacob praised God, that though, as a lonely traveller he had passed over the

Jordan with only his staff, by the grace of God he had become two bands. Now, however, he gets an enlarged vision and sees the two bands becoming a great nation of twelve tribes, who, according to God's promise, are to be the means of blessing to the world (Gen. 28. 3, 4, 14). How wonderfully God's faithfulness is here exhibited! Let us be doubly sure that not one word of God's precious promises to us will ever fail.

.An Important Phrase.

The expression, "the last days" *acharith hayyamim*, have always been taken by the Rabbis as the Messianic era. The famous commentator, Nachmanades, says, "The last days are the days of the Messiah, for to Him Jacob points when he says, 'Until Shiloh come, and unto Him shall be the obedience of the peoples.' Our Rabbis have taught us that Jacob was going to reveal to his sons the time of the end but the Shekinah departed from him; they all consent that the last days are the days of the Messiah."

The expression is an eschatological term, and though it has not always precisely the same significance it is equivalent to the *eth kets* "end time" of Dan. 12. 4, 9, the *en esxatais hemerais* of the apostle.

Delitzsch defines it as "Denoting, not the future course of history that forms the present, but the future which forms the close of history."

It is the furthest point of the prophetic vision, and is usually limited to the speaker's horizon. It is the terminal point to which the entire process of history tends.

Isaiah 2. 2, 4, speaks of it as the time when Christ in the midst of Israel will also be the centre of light and peace to the nations of the world. "And it shall come to pass in the latter days, that the mountain of Jehovah's house shall be established upon the top of the mountains and shall be exalted above the hills; and all nations shall flow unto it. And many peoples shall go and say, Come ye, and let us go up to the mountain of Jehovah, to the house of the God of Jacob, and He will teach us of His ways, and we will walk in His paths, for out of Zion shall go forth the law, and the Word of Jehovah from Jerusalem. And He will judge between the nations, and umpire for many peoples, and they shall beat their swords into ploughshares, and their spears into pruning hooks."

Ezekiel speaks of it as the time of Israel's restoration, and the activities of Gog, king of Magog. "In the latter years (*acharith hashshanim*) thou shalt come into the land that is brought back from the sword, that is gathered out of many peoples, upon the mountains of Israel which have been constantly waste, but is brought forth out of the peoples; and they shall dwell securely all of them. And thou shalt ascend, Thou shalt come like a storm" (Ezek. 38. 8, 9).

Hosea 3. 5 refers it to the time of Israel's reconciliation to their Messiah. "Afterwards shall the children of Israel return and seek Jehovah their God, and David their king, and shall fear Jehovah and His goodness in the latter days."

The Heavenly visitor mentioned in Dan. 10. 14, expresses himself very similarly to Jacob: "I am come to make thee understand what shall befall thy people in the last days." The revelation the angel brings is of a series of events leading up to and embracing the second advent of our Lord. This is also the case with Gen. 49.

Jacob's First-born.

The first son whom Jacob addresses is Reuben. "Thou art my firstborn, my might and the beginning of my strength, pre-eminent in dignity and pre-eminent in power. Unstable as water, thou shalt not have the pre-eminence." It was the custom of those early days for the eldest son to have the priority of right and privilege; this Jacob now takes away from Reuben because of his sin, and gives it to Joseph, whose two sons, Manasseh and Ephraim, became separate tribes (Gen. 48. 5; 1 Chron. 5. 2).

That Jacob attached great importance to the birthright we know from the fact that he was very anxious to obtain it for himself from his brother Esau. He did not think that Reuben was worthy of it.

The Ancient Jerusalem Targum—the Chaldaic Paraphrase—renders Genesis 49. 3, 4,

"Reuben, my firstborn art thou, my strength, and the beginning of my sorrow.

To thee, my son Reuben, would it have pertained to receive three portions above thy brothers, the priesthood, birthright, and kingdom, but because thou hast sinned, the birthright is given to Joseph, the kingdom to Judah, and the High Priesthood to Levi."

By the sinful gratification of a moment, Reuben lost the blessing of ages. It is a terrible thought, but it often happens that a sin, giving pleasure for only a moment, has brought dire consequences upon the sinner himself and upon his posterity for generations afterwards.

Leah, when giving a name to her firstborn son, embodied in it her feeling of joy at giving birth to a male child; hoping it would be the means of winning for her the husband's affection. The proud mother, as our Lord expressed it, remembered "no more the anguish (of childbirth) for joy that a man is born into the world," and with great delight exclaimed, *Re-u-ben*, "See ye a son!"   In her gratitude to God she also applies the same verb to Him, "Jehovah *hath seen* my affliction" (Gen. 29. 32).

Do we not recognise in Reuben a picture of ourselves?   When first created, man enjoyed many privileges, but he lost them all through his sinful conduct, like another firstborn, Esau, who for one morsel of meat sold his birthright and afterwards, when he would have inherited the blessing, he was rejected, for "he found no place for repentance, though he sought it diligently with tears."

Reuben's Lack of Courage.

The instability or weakness of Reuben's character showed itself in his conduct towards Joseph.   Feeling his responsibility as the eldest brother he managed to prevent his death by a subterfuge, by casting him into a pit, intending stealthily to deliver him and take him back to his father, but when he found that, during his absence, Joseph had been sold, he said to his brethren, "The child is not; and I, whither shall I go?"   He then joined them in the deceitful act of dipping Joseph's coat in the blood of a young goat, and telling Jacob that they found it thus.

God graciously overruled it all and brought good out of the evil, according to His purpose, but Reuben did not display the courage of the eldest son, and did not rightfully act up to his responsibility and deliver Joseph.   No wonder that his father, knowing the weakness of his character, would not, later on, entrust Benjamin to his care notwithstanding all his entreaties (Gen. 42. 37, 38).

We need grace and courage honestly and fearlessly

to act up to our convictions that we may enjoy God's approval and blessing.

Important Lessons of the Narrative.

What lessons these interesting narratives teach us! How many men of privilege and promise have had their lives marred and their careers ruined by yielding to temptation that gave them a moment of pleasure!

In this incident of Reuben we see, however, not only human weakness, but also the Divine remedy as indicated by his name, Reuben, "See ye a son," the Child born, the Son given.

The descendants of Reuben did not take the lead in any of the great national events, and did not display any prominence. In the wilderness journey they occupied the centre of the second or southern group of marchers, having Simeon on one side and Gad on the other. According to tradition, on Reuben's standard was portrayed the figure of a man, or son, in harmony with the meaning of his name. Confirmation is claimed for this from the fact that one of the faces of the cherubic figures representing the four leading tribes as they journeyed in the wilderness, was that of a man. The second face being a lion, like the standard of Judah (Gen. 49. 9). The third face— that of an ox, being the standard of Ephraim, which name comes from the same root as the Hebrew word for ox, *par* from *parah*, to be fruitful, or fruit bearing. Of this we have Joseph's explanation (Gen. 41. 52). "And the name of the second (son) called he Ephraim, for God had caused me to be fruitful in the land of my affliction." Play is similarly put upon Ephraim's name in Hosea 13. 15.

The Eagle, or fourth face of the cherub, is a substitute for the serpent (Gen. 49. 17) and is said to have been displayed on the standard of Dan.

Jacob and Moses.

It is helpful to compare Jacob's prediction concerning Reuben with the blessing of Moses (Deut. 33. 6). Moses prays for him, "Let Reuben live and not die, and let not his men be few." According to the Law, Reuben's sin was punishable by death. Does Moses now indicate his pardon, let Reuben live and not die? Knowing that the curse was resting upon the tribe, he, the mediator of the Old Covenant and type of Christ, tenderly intercedes for them. This is the more remarkable because some of the descendants of Reuben were the ringleaders in the rebellion against himself (Num. 16. 1).

Moses the Mediator.

Just as on other occasions Moses pleaded on behalf of Israel, even when God said He would make him into a greater and mightier nation than they were, he prayed, "O Jehovah, longsuffering and of great mercy . . . Pardon, I beseech Thee, the iniquity of this people according to the greatness of Thy mercy." And the response was, "I have pardoned according to thy word" (Num. 14. 12, 18-20. See also Exod. 33. 11-14).

What a picture this is of our great Mediator—the Lord Jesus Christ—interceding on our behalf and procuring for us the pardon and favour of God! Does it not remind us of His prayer on the Cross for those who were putting Him to death, and driving the sharp nails into the tender flesh of His hands and feet, for those who were cruelly reviling Him? "Father, forgive them, for they know not what they do."

Israel, God's First-born.

Jacob's firstborn son, Reuben, is a figure of Israel, God's firstborn (Exod. 4. 22; Jer. 31. 9).

They, too, because of their sins, are now under condemnation and have lost the pre-eminence and privileges that were theirs; but Scripture makes it quite clear that because of the mediation of the Lord Jesus, their Messiah, they will be pardoned, the curse will be removed from them, and they will be restored to their original position of privilege and blessing. How striking! not only are all the tribes of Israel restored to their own land according to the plain prediction of Ezek. 48, but every one of the twelve gates of the heavenly Jerusalem has inscribed upon it one of the names of these tribes, while the foundations of that city have in them the names of the twelve apostles of the Lamb, also all Jews. Similarly, through the Old Testament prophet, the Lord declares "Behold, I have graven thee upon the palms of My hands, thy walls are continually before Me" (Isa. 49. 16).

Be consoled, O penitent one, your sin is a burden on you, it has brought you under condemnation, and your penalty is death. But look to the Saviour, Who died in your stead, that you, like Reuben, may live and not die. For Christ has declared, "he that believeth on Me though he die yet shall he live."

Chapter III

Simeon—Hearing

" Simeon and Levi are brethren,
  Instruments of violence are their barterings ;
  Into their council come not thou, O my soul ;
  In their assembly be thou not united, O my honour ;
  For in their anger they slew a man,
  And in their self-will they hamstringed an ox.
  Cursed be their anger, for it was fierce,
  And their wrath, for it was cruel ;
  I will divide them in Jacob,
  And scatter them in Israel " (Gen. 49. 5-7).

Chapter III

Simeon—Hearing

THE Patriarch addresses his sons in the order of their ages, so after dealing with Reuben, the firstborn, he turned to Simeon and Levi, who were next according to age, these two he linked together in condemnation because of their joint act of cruelty against the people of Shechem.

The Crime Condemned.

Jacob's mind was evidently lingering on this dreadful crime they committed, which must have caused him great grief, and which was the means of disturbing the life of the whole family, for it compelled them all to leave the district where they were happily settled, as we learn from Gen. 34. 30.

"And Jacob said to Simeon and Levi, Ye have troubled me to make me odious to the inhabitants of the land, among the Canaanites, and the Perizzites; and I being few in number, they will gather themselves against me; and I shall be destroyed, I and my house."

The people of the land might easily have taken vengeance on them had not God protected them, as we are told.

"And a terror of God was upon the cities that were round about them, and they did not pursue after the sons of Jacob" (Gen. 35. 5).

Jacob's strongly worded protestation against them so many years after it had happened, clearly shows that he was not thinking merely of the physical disadvantages brought on the family by that act, but more so of the moral wrong they committed which left such an ugly stain upon their soul and character. This terrible sin against God and man he could not forget.

" Simeon and Levi are brethren,
Instruments of violence are their barterings.
Into their council come not thou, O my soul,
In their assembly be thou not united, O my honour."

Before God and men, as it were, the Patriarch dissociates himself from this wicked crime of his two sons, and his character has come down to posterity unbesmirched by it.

" For in their anger they slew a man,
And in their self-will they hamstringed an ox.
Cursed be their anger, for it was fierce,
And their wrath, for it was cruel."

God Looks at the Heart.

Their anger is cursed because it led them on to commit murder, and their wilfulness to acts of cruelty. This has often been the case with people.

John tells us similarly, "Whosoever hateth his brother is a murderer" (1 John 3. 15). Because anger and hatred being frequently the cause and forerunner of the crime, God, who knows our desires and intentions, and to what they tend, counts these passions as the crimes which result from them.

" I will divide them in Jacob,
And scatter them in Israel."

In Jacob's vision the persons merge into the family, and the family expands into the tribe, and becomes a unit of the nation, he therefore deals with the tribes as with their personal progenitors, the one name represents the two.

Levi was separated from Simeon and dispersed among the nation. In the journeyings through the wilderness he had his place apportioned by the side of his elder brother, Reuben.

The Simeonites were greatly diminished in numbers during their journey in the wilderness. At the first census (Num. 1. 23), their number was 59,300, in the second census (Num. 26. 14), they were reduced to 22,200; they thus decreased by 37,100, that is by more than half. It is generally taken that their great diminution was the result of their sin in connection with Baal-Peor, as one of their princes, Zimri, the son of Salu, was specially involved in it (Num. 25. 14). There was also the plague on account of the Rebellion of Korah (Num. 16. 49).

Simeon's Inheritance.

It is in harmony with Jacob's condemnation of Simeon that when the land of promise was apportioned to the tribes, Simeon had only allotted to him a section in Judah's possession, and that, right to the extreme south. "Out of the part of the children of Judah was the inheritance of the children of Simeon; for the portion of Judah was too much for them, therefore the children of Simeon had inheritance in the midst of their inheritance" (Joshua 19. 9). It would also seem that even from that which they had, some of the towns reverted to Judah again, for in 1 Kings 19. 3, Beersheba is said to belong to Judah. Ziklag, another of their towns, seems also to have been in the private possession of David, given to him by Achish, king of Gath (1 Sam. 27. 6).

Simeon's inheritance was evidently insufficient for them, for we read that some of them migrated to Gedor, and another five hundred men went to Mount Seir, and there they smote the remnant of the Amale-

kites that had escaped, and they dwelt in their places
(1 Chron. 4. 39-43). The descendants of these five
hundred on Mount Seir were evidently not affected
by the Babylonian Captivity, for they were still there
when the Chronicles were written in the days of Ezra.
(1 Chron. 4. 43).

In the days of Josiah the Simeonites are counted
with the people of Ephraim, Manasseh, and Naphtali
(2 Chron. 34. 6). All this goes to show how accurately
Jacob's prediction was fulfilled. They were indeed
divided in Jacob and dispersed in Israel.

Simeon—Hearing.

Moses, in blessing the tribes, does not mention
Simeon. Neither does Deborah mention them among
some of the other tribes, as their territory lay in the
extreme south of the land.

Simeon means "hearing." Leah gave this name
to her second son, exclaiming, "Jehovah heard that
I am hated" (*i.e.*, not loved), hoping again that this
time Jacob will show her greater affection. This
name, however, expresses the truth that God hears
the cry of His children and goes far beyond Leah's
application. It is also true to our experience.

Simeon thus takes his place among the other tribes
in the restored land, according to Ezek. 48. The
prophet changes Simeon's territory from the extreme
south, and places him between Benjamin, on the
north, and Issachar, on the south. His name is also
included among the tribes that are sealed in Rev. 7.
Another exhibition of God's wonderful love and
grace.

The Psalmist speaks of God as the prayer-hearing
God, "O Thou that hearest prayer, unto Thee shall
all flesh come" (Psa. 65. 2). It is God's characteristic to hear our cry and deliver. Concerning Israel,

God graciously promises, "And it shall come to pass, that before they call I will answer; and while they are yet speaking I will hear" (Isa. 65. 24). With Micah of old, we may exclaim, with the greatest confidence, "As for me I will look unto Jehovah; I will wait for the God of my salvation, my God will hear me" (Micah 7. 7).

God not only hears and answers our prayers, He also listens with interest to all our conversations. This is beautifully illustrated in Mal. 3. 13-17. He hears and reproves the hard words spoken against Him, "Your words have been stout against Me, saith Jehovah. Yet ye say, What have we spoken against Thee? Ye have said, It is vain to serve God; and what profit is it that we have kept His charge, and that we have walked mournfully before Jehovah of Hosts? And now we call the proud happy; yea, they that work wickedness are built up, yea, they tempt God and escape."

These were the murmurings of the people, but while they were complaining that God was uninterested and indifferent to what goes on, He shows that He was both interested and concerned; He has taken note of the harsh words they have spoken of Him.

He listens attentively, moreover, to all that the righteous say about Him.

"They that feared Jehovah spake often one with another, and Jehovah hearkened and heard it, and a book of remembrance was written before Him, for them that feared Jehovah, and that thought upon His Name."

"The Hebrew word *yakshebh*, here translated hearkened," would perhaps be better rendered "listened attentively," the result being that *yishma*, "He heard."

The same expression is used by Isaiah in depicting

a watchman standing on a high tower, peering into the distance to descry the enemy coming from afar, and listening with great attention, in order to catch the slightest sound coming from the direction of the enemy. The Hebrew is *hikshibh kashebh rabh kashebh*, and is translated, "He hearkened diligently with great heed" (Isa. 21. 7).

The picture is of one straining to listen, almost with his hand to his ear that he may not miss the slightest whisper of the speaker, so interested is God in all His children say and think about Him. How condescending! Yea, He not only hears, but keeps a permanent record of it all, "And a book of remembrance was written before Him."

Moreover, He bestows upon them an adequate reward for it, "And they shall be Mine, saith Jehovah of Hosts, in the day when I make up My private treasure, and I will deal compassionately with them as a man deals compassionately with his own son that serveth him." God is not unmindful of His faithful servants.

CHAPTER IV

Levi—Joining

" And of Levi he said :
Thy Thummim and thy Urim are with Thy godly one,
Whom Thou didst prove at Massah,
With whom Thou didst strive at the waters of
    Meribah ;
Who said of his father and mother,
I have not seen him,
Neither did he acknowledge his brethren,
Nor knew his own children ;
For they have observed Thy Word,
And did keep Thy covenant.
They shall teach Jacob Thine ordinances
And Israel Thy Law ;
They shall put incense before Thee,
And whole burnt offerings upon Thine Altar.
Bless, O Jehovah, his substance,
And accept the work of his hands ;
Smite through the loins of them that rise up against
    him,
And of them that hate him,
That they rise not again " (Deut. 33. 8-11).

CHAPTER IV

Levi—Joining

THE name Levi comes from the root *Lavah*, "to join closely," as we see from the play put upon it by his mother at the time of his birth, when with greater confidence than before, she said, "This time will my husband be joined unto me because I have borne him three sons" (Gen. 29. 34).

Levi was closely associated with Simeon in the wicked crime against the Shechemites. As we have seen, Jacob calls them brethren, and because they were linked together in crime he links them together in condemnation, while he dissociates himself from their secret council in planning the treacherous act, and from the company of those who carried it out; and moreover, he separates and disperses them in Israel. We have also noticed how literally this was fulfilled in Simeon. In the case of Levi this was also carried into effect, but was overruled for good; because after the Israelites went astray in the worship of the golden calf, the tribe of Levi, at the call of Moses, gathered themselves unto him, and at the word of command were ready to carry out God's sentence against the idolators. "And Moses said, Consecrate yourselves to-day unto Jehovah, yea, every man against his son and against his brother, that He may bestow upon you a blessing this day" (Exod. 36. 26-29). This was verified to them; their condemnation by Jacob was changed into commendation by Moses. They put God first, before their nearest and dearest. We, too, must love and obey Christ more than our fathers and mothers, sisters and brothers, in order to be worthy of Him, and to enjoy His blessing.

God's Overruling Grace.

Levi's loyal attachment to Jehovah thus draws out the benediction of Moses and exhibits God's readiness to forgive and to overrule on our behalf, bringing good out of evil.

The sentence that they should be dispersed among the rest of the nation was carried out, for the Levites had no separate tribal territory allotted to them, as we are told in Josh. 13. 33, "Unto the tribe of Levi, Moses gave no inheritance; Jehovah was their inheritance, as He spake unto them." Forty-eight cities and their surrounding suburbs were appointed for them from all the other tribes.

This dispersion in Israel was overruled for the highest blessing of the whole nation as well as for themselves; for they became the priestly tribe, and the teachers of the people, according to the prediction of Moses, "They shall teach Jacob Thine ordinances, and Israel Thy Law; they shall put incense before Thee, and whole burnt offering upon Thine altar." As the priestly tribe with the Urim and Thummim they represented God to the people, and with incense and offerings they represented the people before God. A type of Christ.

The prophet, Malachi, in denouncing the priests of his day for their negligence in the service of God, and their impiety, declared that God would curse their blessings. It was their prerogative to pronounce the Aaronic benediction upon the people, but these would be turned into maledictions and work out for their disadvantage. This is frequently the case with those whose conduct is opposed to God; the very things on which they set their hearts turn out to their hurt and loss. But it was just the contrary in the early history of the Levites. As a reward of their faithfulness their loss in not having a compact piece of land as the other tribes had, proved to be for the spiritual benefit of the entire nation.

We also may be sure that God is not unrighteous to forget the work and labour of love of His servants. He is a rewarder of them that diligently seek Him.

Moses outlines the ministry of the priestly section of the tribe; they were the bearers of the Urim and Thummim on their breast, and enquired of the Lord His will and direction for the people. They were, further, the instructors of the nation, teaching "Jacob his ordinances and Israel His Law." And in the capacity of the mediator they placed the incense before the Lord and offered burnt offerings on His altar.

How wonderful is God's grace that turns sinners into saints! Levi, bitter and revengeful, ready to destroy a whole township, yet his descendants, illumined by the Spirit, acting as mediators between sinful men and a holy God, dispersed over all the land, instructing the people in the Law of the Lord.

The greater section of the tribe who were not of Aaronic descent were also used in the service of God, assisting the Priests and leading the people in the Tabernacle and Temple worship. We think of the names of Asaph, Heman, and Jeduthun who composed some of the Psalms and led Israel in the singing.

Heroes of the Tribe.

What a galaxy of great names the Levitical tribe produced during Israel's history! Moses, the illustrious leader and Law-giver; Aaron, the first high priest; Phinehas, the averter of God's wrath; Samuel, the founder of the schools of the prophets, specially characterised as a man of prayer. "Samuel among such as call upon His Name" (Psa. 99. 6); Jehoiada, the great reformer, who purged the land of Baal worship, protected the life of young Joash, and placed him on the throne; Jeremiah and Ezekiel, the faithful prophets at the beginning of the Exile, who dared to withstand king and people. Then, during the time of the second Temple, the brave Maccabean family* who, with a handful of men, obtained the wonderful victories over the great armies of Antiochus Epiphanes, and restored the Temple worship. Finally, John the Baptist, of whom our Lord said, that, "among those born of women there hath not risen a greater than John the Baptist." Jewish tradition says that Elijah was also of Aaronic descent.

Nevertheless, the tribe of Levi has fallen far short of their high privileges. With the declension of the nation the priests became lax in their ministry. The divine ordinances which they had to perform, and which, as types of our blessed Lord were of such sublime import, became to them mere formalities. How prone to evil is the heart of man!

There was a great blot made on the name of Levi by a descendant of that tribe, who was one of the first to introduce among the Danites, images in the worship of Jehovah (Judges 17. 7; 18. 31), thus making it easy for Jeroboam, the son of Nebat, to establish in Dan the worship of the calves (1 Kings 12. 28-30). This stain becomes more regrettable because it

---

*The actual name of this priestly family was Chashmonai. The title of Maccabeans is said to have been given them because in their wars against the armies of Antiochus Epiphanes. they had inscribed on the ensigns, or standards, that they carried on the battlefield, four words taken from the song of Moses (Exod. 15. 11), *Mi chamochah ba-alim Jehovah*, "Who among the gods is like unto Thee, O Jehovah." The Hebrew word *Machbi*, the singular for Maccabees, is of four letters, the initials of the above four words.

One can quite understand how they would be encouraged by these words and spurred on to deeds of bravery in what they regarded as the battle of the Lord against an enemy that compelled them to forsake the worship of Jehovah and to serve heathen deities.

besmirches the fair name of Moses. Judges 18. 30 reads: "And the children of Dan set up the graven image, and Jonathan, the son of Gershom, the son of Manasseh, he and his sons were priests unto the tribe of Dan unto the day that the land was taken away into captivity." But who was this Jonathan, who is here called the son of Gershom, the son of Manasseh? In the original the word Manasseh has the letter *n* suspended, as though it is an addition that does not belong to it, and without it the Hebrew word reads Moses, so that Jonathan was the grandson of Moses, but the Rabbis explain that in order not to tarnish the splendour of Moses' name the letter *n* was inserted halfway in the middle of the word, that instead of Moses it should read Manasseh, to link him with the idolatrous king of Judah, who was of the same character as himself (2 Kings 21. 1-7).

The prophet Malachi charges the Levites with disobeying and dishonouring Jehovah, and offering polluted bread upon His altar, and presenting to God the blind, the lame, and the sick. Having healthy males among their flock, yet sacrificing blemished animals, a practice forbidden by the Law. He further asks them, "Who is among you that would shut the door for nought? neither do ye kindle fire on My altar for nought," and then declares, "I have no pleasure in you, saith Jehovah of Hosts" (Mal. 1. 10). Chapter 2. 4-7 brings before them the Ideal Priest, a picture that in its entirety is only true of Christ. "The law of truth was in His mouth, and unrighteousness was not found in His lips: He walked with Me in peace and uprightness and turned many away from iniquity. For the priest's lips should keep knowledge, and they should ask the law at His mouth, for He is the messenger (literally, the angel) of Jehovah of Hosts."

This evidently has Phinehas as a background (Num. 25. 11-13), but he himself as Israel's High Priest was a type of Christ, and actually neither he nor any other human being has reached up to the high standard of these verses; of our Lord alone are they entirely true.

It is also very noteworthy, that after bringing the terrible indictment against the priests, and predicting their rejection, the prophet gets a vision of the Coming Messiah, and sees Him, as a refiner of precious metals, purging and purifying the sons of Levi, making them again fit to perform their service in a restored temple worship, and a re-established priesthood acceptable to God. "Behold, I send My messenger, and he shall prepare the way before Me, and the Lord Whom ye seek will suddenly come to His temple, even the Messenger (Angel) of the covenant Whom ye desire, Behold, He cometh, saith Jehovah of Hosts. But who can abide the day of His coming? and who shall stand when He appeareth? for He is like a refiner's fire, and like fuller's soap, and He will purify the sons of Levi, and refine them as gold and silver, and they shall offer unto Jehovah offerings in righteousness. Then shall the offering of Judah and Jerusalem be pleasant unto Jehovah, as in the days of old and as in former years" (Mal. 3. 1-4).

The Lawgiver invokes a blessing upon their work and substance, that God may accept them, and finally give them the victory over their enemies (Deut. 33. 11). This will find its fulfilment in the end-time, as is indicated by Malachi 3.

What is true of Levi as a tribe in the midst of Israel, is also true of Israel as a people amongst the nations, both have had their call and their rejection. Both will also have their restoration.

To Israel it was said, "If ye will obey My voice

indeed, and keep My covenant, then ye shall be Mine own possession above all peoples; for all the earth is Mine. And ye shall be unto Me a kingdom of priests and an holy nation" (Exod. 19. 5, 6). Alas! Israel has not obeyed God's voice and has not kept His covenant. As a kingdom of priests they were intended to bring blessing to the nations of the earth, but in that they have utterly failed.

"This people have I formed for Myself; they shall show forth My praise," is God's declaration. Then the prophet continues, "But thou hast not called upon Me, O Jacob, but thou hast been weary of Me, O Israel, thou hast not brought Me the sheep of thy burnt offerings; neither hast thou honoured Me with thy sacrifices . . . thou hast brought Me no sweet cane with money, neither hast thou filled Me with the fat of thy sacrifices." He nevertheless declares, "I, even I, am He that blotteth out thy transgressions for Mine own sake; and will not remember thy sins" (Isa. 43. 21-25).

Israel as a nation, like the tribe of Levi, will be purged by fire and purified, "I will bring the (remaining) third through the fire, and will refine them as silver is refined, and will test them as gold is tested; they shall call upon my Name and I will hear them; I will say it is My people, and they shall say, Jehovah is my God" (Zech. 13. 9).

In their renewed relationship with God, Israel will fulfil His original purpose for them, they will be the kingdom of priests, and the holy nation they were meant to be. As He sees them in their restored condition the prophet exclaims, "Ye shall be named the priests of Jehovah; men shall call you the ministers of our God" (Isa. 61. 6). Picturesquely they shall also be called "Trees of righteousness, the planting of Jehovah that He might be glorified" (ibid. v. 3).

CHAPTER V

Judah—Praise

" Judah, thou art he whom thy brethren shall praise ;
Thine hand shall be on the neck of thine enemies ;
Thy father's sons shall bow down before thee.
Judah is a lion's whelp ;
From the prey, my son, thou art gone up ;
He stooped down, he couched as a lion,
And as a roaring lion ;
Who shall rouse him up ! " (Gen. 49. 8, 9).

CHAPTER V

Judah—Praise

THE blessing of Judah, like that of his elder brothers, commences with his own experience, looks on to the future of the tribe, and finds its highest fulfilment in his noblest son, the Lord Jesus Christ.

In the tribe of Levi we have a double type of Christ, (*a*) the Prophet, making known the will of God to the people, teaching Jacob His ordinances and Israel His law; and (*b*) the Priest, bringing the sweet-smelling incense of His life to God, and the whole burnt offering of His atoning death for God's acceptance. In the tribe of Judah, following Levi, we have, therefore, very suitably set forth the King Who shall reign and prosper.

Meaning of the Name.

"Judah, thou art he whom thy brethren shall praise."

Here again play is put on the name Judah, Jehovah is praised, as we see from Gen. 29. 35. When Leah gave birth to this, her fourth son, she exclaimed with gratitude, "This time will I praise Jehovah, therefore she called his name Judah."

It was Judah who gave his name to the Jewish people (another form of it is Judean). Paul seems to have the meaning of this name in mind when he writes: "He is a Jew which is one inwardly, and circumcision is that of the heart, in the spirit and not in the letter; whose praise is not of men but of God" (Rom. 2. 29).   To Judah it was said, "Thy brethren shall praise thee," but it is more important to have the praise of God than the praise of the brethren.   Play is thus put on the name of Judah, or Jew.

How wonderfully we see God's guidance even in the names of these typical men!   It is not so much for Judah that we have to praise God.   It is specially for Judah's great Son that our deepest praise should be given to God.   It was in the tribe of Judah that it pleased the Lord to provide the mould in which the humanity of Christ should be cast.

Reference to Judah Himself.

Judah was by no means perfect, but he had some good traits of character.   It was at his suggestion that Joseph was not put to death by the brethren. His words must have touched all their hearts as he pleaded:

"What profit is it if we slay our brother and conceal his blood?   Come, and let us sell him to the Ishmaelites, and let not our hand be upon him, for he is our brother, our flesh; and his brethren hearkened unto him" (Gen. 37. 26, 27).

He thus saved Joseph's life.

He also seems to have had greater influence with his father than his brothers.   As we noticed before, it was to his earnest pleading that Jacob yielded and sent Benjamin with them to Egypt.   His words are pregnant with meaning.   After his father refused to listen to Reuben and the other sons, Judah approached him and said:

"Send the lad with me, and we will arise and go; that we may live, and not die, both we and thou, and also our little ones.   *I will be surety for him; of my hand shalt thou require him.*   If I bring him not unto thee, and set him before thee, then let me bear the blame for ever" (Gen. 43. 8, 9). Jacob then consented.

It is thus that the Lord Jesus made Himself responsible for us to the Father. No one else could possibly have carried out the important mission of preserving our lives, *"That we may live and not die."* This is indicated in a great verse (Jer. 30. 21).

"And their noble one (*addiro,* singular) shall be of themselves, and their ruler shall proceed from the midst of them; and I will cause Him to draw near and He shall approach unto me; for who is this that made his heart surety to approach unto Me? saith Jehovah."

The very Hebrew expression *arav* that Judah used to Jacob is here repeated. It is Christ, the Noble One out of the midst of Judah, Who had approached His Father on our behalf and given Him the necessary pledge for our safety.

This is further brought out in Gen. 44. 18-34, where Judah pleads so eloquently for his youngest brother; He tells Joseph that he had made himself surety unto the father for the lad, and offers to remain as a bond-servant instead of him, so that he should be freed. Is not this what the Lord Jesus has done on our behalf? He, indeed, not only *offered* to become a servant, but actually took upon Him the form of a bondman in our stead. The Greek *doulos* is, of course, the equivalent of the Hebrew *eved* used by Judah, and is a title frequently used for Christ. It speaks of Him, Who,

Though He was rich yet for our sake He became poor, that we, through His poverty might become rich.

We are told (1 Chron. 5. 2) that Judah prevailed above his brethren. Numerically they were the strongest tribe, and from early in their history they took a leading part in the affairs of the nation. They marched foremost before the Ark in the wilderness, having Nahshon, one of our Lord's ancestors, as prince leader (Matt. 1. 4; Num. 2. 3). After the death of Joshua, Judah was commanded by the Oracle of the Urim to be the first in attacking the enemy (Judges 1. 2). Thus, in the strength of Judah's character lay latent the vigour of the future tribe.

Great Men of Judah.

The tribe of Judah had many worthy men who foreshadowed the Lord Jesus. There was Bezaleel (meaning, in the shade or protection of God) who, though not a Levite, was nevertheless

"Filled with the Spirit of God, in wisdom, in understanding, and in knowledge, and in all manner of workmanship. And to devise skilful work, to work in gold, in silver, and in brass,"

for the furniture of the Tabernacle, to make it a fit dwelling-house for God. In this he also typified the Lord Jesus, Who is building the spiritual tabernacle composed of living stones.

Caleb the Warrior.

Then there is Caleb (meaning the valiant), the faithful hero who with Joshua insisted, in opposition to the other spies, that the Israelites should go up and possess the land. Forty-five years later the Lord enabled him, as a reward of his fidelity, to play a principal part in the conquest of Palestine, when he conquered Kirjath Arba—the city of the giants—driving out the sons of Anak, Sheshai, Ahiman, and Talmai. He said to Joshua:

"I am this day eighty-five years old. As yet I am as strong this day as I was in the day that Moses sent me, as my strength was then, even so it is now, for war, and going out and coming in. Now therefore, give me the hill country whereof Jehovah spake in that day. Thou heardest how the Anakims were there and cities great and fortified" (Joshua 14. 7-12).

Does he not thus prefigure Him Who, as the "Mighty One," shall one day go forth conquering and to conquer, and the peoples shall fall under Him? (Psa. 45. 3-5).

Boaz the Kinsman.

We also think of Boaz, the gracious kinsman redeemer, who by marriage united himself to Ruth, the Gentile who had been alienated from the commonwealth of Israel and estranged from the covenant of promise, but who was brought near, and made a fellow-citizen with the saints and of the household of God.

David, Solomon, and the Kings.

Then there was, of course, David, the beloved, the warrior king, and his son, "the man of rest," Solomon (*Shelomo*) by name—to whom was given (*Shalom*) peace and tranquillity. These two kings together setting forth Him, Who, after subduing His enemies, will set up a reign of peace and righteousness, when every man shall sit "under his vine and under his fig tree; and no one shall make him afraid.

There was also King Hezekiah, the reformer, and indeed the whole Davidic dynasty, each king being a pledge and earnest of King Messiah, the Divine Ruler to come.

Other Heroes.

Another was Benaiah, the son of Jehoiada—the valiant man of Kabzeel, a town in Judah, mighty in the battles of the Lord, who slew the two giants of Moab, and killed a lion in its den on a snowy day. Thus prefiguring Him, Who, "having despoiled the principalities and the powers, made a show of them openly, triumphing over them in it" (Col. 2. 15).

Nor must we forget Daniel, "the man greatly beloved," and his faithful companions, Hananiah, Mishael, and Azariah, all children of Judah, bearing testimony to the God of Israel at a time of great national declension.

Jewish tradition also makes Isaiah the prophet to be of the tribe of Judah and family of David.

Christ's Surpassing Glory.

All these heroes, however, sink into insignificance before the greatest Son of that tribe, the Lord Jesus, in Whom this sublime prophecy finds its highest fulfilment.

"Thou art He Whom Thy brethren shall praise . . .
Thy father's sons shall bow down before Thee."

Our Lord combines in Himself, in the highest degree, all the noble qualities and offices of the men of Judah. Were they kings? To Him is given

"Dominion and glory, and a kingdom, that all peoples and nations and languages should serve Him" (Dan. 7. 14).

Their rule lasted but a brief period at the longest, but

"His dominion is an everlasting dominion which shall not pass away, and His Kingdom that which shall not be destroyed" (ibid.).

They reigned over only a small strip of territory,

"His dominion shall be from sea to sea, and from the river to the ends of the earth" (Zech. 9. 10).

Were any of them prophets? They only foreshadowed Him Who revealed not only God's purpose, but also God's Person.

Did any of them perform valiant deeds? Which of their achievements can possibly be compared with the wonderful accomplishments of Christ on the Cross, Who by dying "abolished death and hath brought life and immortality to light through the Gospel"? (2 Tim. 1. 10).

Did any of them achieve glory and greatness? Christ more, for God hath

"Raised Him from the dead, and set Him at His own right hand in the Heavenlies, far above all principality, and power, and might, and dominion, and every name that is named, not only in this world, but also in that which is to come, and hath put all things under His feet" (Eph. 1. 20-22).

The Lion of the Tribe of Judah.

Judah is here compared to a young lion gone up from the prey, and as a grown lion couching dauntlessly, no one daring to rouse him up. Some translate *labhi*, "lioness." The picture would then be of a lioness couching to protect her young.

Balaam similarly likens Israel to an invincible lion in a couching, fearless attitude, evidently connecting it with the rule of Christ. The scene is cast in the reign of King Messiah, Who shall be higher than Agag (or Gog), and Whose Kingdom shall be exalted (Num. 24. 7-9).

Micah also referring to the same time, predicts that the remnant of Jacob shall be among many peoples, as a lion amongst the cattle of the wood, and as a young lion amongst the folds of sheep, when the Ruler of Bethlehem Ephratah shall stand and feed as a shepherd in the strength of Jehovah His God (Micah 5. 2-8).

There is a tradition that Judah, numerically the

strongest of the tribes, in the wilderness journey had emblazoned upon his banner the figure of a lion.

The symbolism of Revelation 5, where our Lord is portrayed as the Lion of the tribe of Judah, is evidently based on Gen. 49. In Revelation 5 the Lord Jesus combines in Himself the characteristics of the lamb in regard to His suffering and atoning work, and those of the lion as setting forth His Kingship and strength. Even as the lamb He is portrayed as having seven horns, "perfect strength," and seven eyes, "perfect vision"—Omnipotence and Omniscience.

Our Lord Receiving Divine Worship.

Jacob further indicates that Judah was to receive the homage of his brethren.

"Thy hand shall be upon the neck of thine enemies;
    Thy father's sons shall bow down before thee."

As far as is recorded this was never verified to Judah himself, and only partially realised by the tribe. It will, however, be abundantly fulfilled in the experience of the Messiah.

The word rendered "bow down," in Gen. 49. 8, is frequently translated "worship," and Rev. 5 gives us a wonderful picture of the Lord Jesus—the Lion of the tribe of Judah—receiving the worship and the praise of the Heavenly host.

Three concentric circles pay Him homage and adoration. First, the four living creatures, having each one a harp and golden bowl full of incense, which are the prayers of the saints, fall down before Him and they sing a new song,

"Worthy art Thou to take the book,
    And to open the seals thereof;
    For Thou wast slain."

Then an enlarged circle of heavenly beings, ten

thousand times ten thousand, and thousands of
thousands of angels, sing their sevenfold doxology,

"Worthy is the Lamb that hath been slain to receive
the power, and riches, and wisdom, and might,
and honour, and glory, and blessing. "

And finally, a still larger circle express universal
homage :

"And every creature which is in Heaven, and on
the earth, and under the earth, and in the sea,
and all that are in them heard I saying,
The blessing, and the honour, and the glory, and
the dominion, be unto Him that sitteth upon the
Throne, and unto the Lamb for ever and ever. "

Thus will Jacob's prophecy be exhaustively fulfilled, when he himself, Leah and Judah, as well as
the whole of that tribe, join with their brethren in
this universal doxology to God and the Lamb. We
long for the time when our Lord shall thus be highly exalted and shall have given to Him the Name that is
above every name ;

"That in the Name of Jesus every knee shall bow,
of things in Heaven and things on earth, and
things under the earth, and every tongue shall
confess that Jesus Christ is Lord to the glory of
God the Father" (Phil. 2. 9-11).

Zion

THE Lord hath afflicted His Zion,
  The city He loved so well;
Where He deign'd, like a couching lion,
  In glory and strength to dwell.
And why hath Jehovah forsaken
  The place of His ancient throne;
His Vine from the wilderness taken,
  To flourish for Him alone?

Ah! deem not the Holy One cruel;
  Had Solyma loved His will,
She had sparkled the costliest jewel,
  The beauty of nations, still;
The Lord had been her Defender,
  And she, the queen of the earth,
In holiness, freedom and splendour,
  Had gloried in Shiloh's birth.

But she fell—and her crown of glory
  Was struck from her rebel brow;
And with feet all wounded and gory,
  She wanders in exile now.
Yet, sad one, distrust not our pity;
  Tho' some may wring out thy tears,
We will weep for the Holy City,
  And sorrow o'er former years.

Thou art stricken, dethroned, and lowly,
  Bereft of a home on earth,
Yet still to our hearts thou art Holy,
  Thou land of Messiah's birth!
He sprang from thy chosen of daughters,
  His star o'er thy hills arose,
He bathed in thy soft flowing waters,
  And wept o'er thy coming woes.

He wept, Who in secret yet lingers,
  With yearnings of heart, o'er thee ;
He, He Whom thy blood-sprinkled fingers
  Once nailed to the cursed tree.
Dark deed ! it was thine to afflict Him ;
  Yet longs His soul for the day
When thou, in the blood of thy Victim.
  Shalt wash thy deep stains away.

Thou land of the Cross, and the Glory,
  Whose brightness at last will shine
Afar through the earth—what a story
  Of darkness and light is thine !
He died as a Lamb—as a Lion,
  He spares thee, nor can forget
His desolate exile of Zion ;
  He waits to be gracious yet.

                The late Sir EDWARD DENNY, Bart.
                From *The Believers' Magazine.*

CHAPTER VI

Judah (continued)

" The tribal sceptre shall not depart from Judah,
Nor a law-giver from between his feet, until Shiloh come ;
And unto him shall be the obedience of the peoples.
Binding his foal unto the vine,
And his ass's colt unto the choice vine,
He washes his garments in wine,
And his vesture in the blood of grapes.
His eyes (are) redder than wine,
And his teeth whiter than milk."   (Genesis 49. 8, 12).

" And this is the blessing of Judah ; and he said,
Hear, Jehovah, the voice of Judah,
And bring him unto his people.
His hands shall be great (mighty) for him,
And Thou shalt be a help against his adversaries."
(Deut. 33. 7).

CHAPTER VI

Judah (continued)

WHILE the whole of this sublime prophecy leads on to Christ, the 10th verse especially points, as with a finger, to Him upon Whom depend the blessing and prosperity, not only of the tribe of Judah, but also of all mankind.

"The Tribal sceptre shall not depart from Judah,
Nor a law-giver from between his feet,
Until Shiloh come,
And unto Him shall be the obedience of the peoples."

Christ is the Shiloh, the tranquiliser, or rest-giver to the weary and heavy laden who come to Him (Matt. 11. 28). Majestic and powerful as the lion of the tribe of Judah, He is also gracious and gentle as a lamb, and He uses His great strength for the purpose of peace.

"In His days shall the righteous flourish,
And abundance of peace till the moon be no more" (Psa. 72. 7).

"Jacob shall return and be in rest, and be tranquil,
And none shall make him afraid" (Jer. 30. 10).

The ancient Rabbis, though not agreeing amongst themselves as to the root meaning of Shiloh, were almost unanimous in applying the term to the Messiah. Rabbi Solomon Yizchaki, a great opponent of the Christianity of his day, interpreted Shiloh as "King Messiah, Whose is the Kingdom."

All three Chaldaic paraphrases that date back to the time of Christ refer it to the Messiah.

Onkelos paraphrases the verse, "A ruler shall not pass away from the house of Judah, nor a scribe from his children's children for ever, even until Messiah comes, and Him will the peoples obey."

Similarly, the Jerusalem Targum, "Kings shall not cease from the house of Judah, nor scribes that teach the law from his children's children, until that time that Messiah comes, and all the kingdoms of the earth shall serve Him.   How beautiful is King Messiah Who is to arise from the house of Judah."

In this prophetic vision multitudes of his noble descendants pass, as it were, before the Patriarch in review, and his gaze falls upon the noblest of them all standing as a conspicuous figure in the midst of the tribe, and in the centre of their history.

The Tribal Rod.

The Hebrew word *Shebhet*, translated "sceptre," like its English equivalent, primarily means "staff" (Latin *sceptrum*, Greek *skeptron-skepto*, to lean).   It is translated once, "pin;" twice, "staff;" ten times "sceptre;" thirty-four times "rod;" one hundred and forty-one times "tribe." This *usus loquendi* shows clearly its meaning.

Primarily the rod was used by the head of the family, and came to be regarded as an emblem of power vested in the person who bore it (Amos 1. 5). From the family it passed over to the tribe (Num. 17. 2).   From the tribe it came to represent the nation (Zech. 10. 11). Finally the national staff became the kingly sceptre (Isa. 14. 5; Esther 4. 11).

In Gen. 49. 10 Jacob is dealing with Judah as a separate tribe, the rod is here, therefore, the tribal sceptre and not the national.

While the regal sceptre of the nation passed away with Zedekiah, the last king of the Davidic dynasty, the tribal distinction of Judah did not depart till Christ came (see Ezek. 21. 25-27).

From the destruction of Jerusalem by Nebuchadnezzar, to this day, no one of the tribe of Judah has sat on the throne of David. During the Babylonian exile the Jews retained their tribal distinction, and their princes, some of whom returned to Jerusalem, as Zerubbabel, for instance. Under the Persian and Grecian rulers the Jews had their own judicial, and in great measure, administrative power; but no King.

In the time of the Seleucidae and the Asmonean family (Mattathias 137 B.C., to Hyrcanus 40 B.C.), there was no Judean king. The Asmonean Rulers were of the tribe of Levi. The Herods, again, were of Idumean descent. The Jews had, nevertheless, many political rights. It was not till eleven years after the birth of Christ, when Archelaus was deposed and Coponius was appointed Roman procurator that Judea became a Roman province. The right of putting anyone to death was then taken away from the Sanhedrim.

At Christ's return, when "The Lord God shall give unto Him the throne of His father David (Isa. 9. 7; Luke 1. 32), the sceptre, tribal, national, and regal, will be restored to Judah again, yea, in the hand of their great Son, our Lord, the sceptre will become universal, for "all peoples, nations and languages shall serve Him," and "His dominion shall be from sea to sea, and from the river to the ends of the earth" (Dan. 7. 14; Zech. 9. 10).

Shiloh a Person.

Some have tried to whittle away this remarkable prophecy by explaining that Shiloh refers to the township in Ephraim where the Tabernacle was placed for a time, but this cannot be the meaning of it as the supremacy of Judah over the other tribes did not commence till after Shiloh was forsaken (Psa. 78. 60, 67, 68), when David became king Joshua was an Ephraimite, Samuel, a Levite, Saul, a Benjamite.

Of the Judges before David, Othniel was of Judah, but all the remainder seem to have belonged to the other tribes. Ehud was a Benjamite, Shamgar was probably of the tribe of Naphtali, as was certainly Barak. Gideon was of Manasseh, Tola of Issachar, Jair the Gileadite was probably of Manasseh, as was evidently Jephthah. Ibzan must have been of Zebulun, as his native town was Bethlehem, not in Ephratah, but a small place in Zebulun. Elon is called a Zebulonite, Abdon was an Ephraimite, Samson a Danite. Eli and Samuel were Levites.

An eminent expositor remarks on this verse: "Many modern critics translate 'until He come to Shiloh,' but this is to be rejected, first as being contrary to all ancient versions; and secondly, as turning sense into nonsense. The town of Shiloh was in the tribe of Ephraim, and we know of no way in which Judah ever went thither. The ark was for a time at Shiloh, but the place lost all importance . . . long before Judah took the leading part in the commonwealth of Israel."—(PAYNE SMITH).

Some object to the Messianic interpretation of this prophecy on the ground that the time of the patriarchs was too early in history for Messianic predictions. The fact is, however, that the promise of a Deliverer is contemporaneous with mankind. It was made to our first parents as soon as they fell from grace. The seed of the woman was to bruise the head of the serpent and in the act was Himself to be bruised in the heel, that is, be wounded temporarily and not permanently, as was the case in His contest with Satan, for our Lord triumphed over death and the grave.

We next get an indication of it in Noah's pronouncement concerning his sons immediately after the Flood. Canaan, representing the Hamitic branch of the human race, was cursed. To Japhet was promised material prosperity (an enlargement), but Shem's blessing consisted in his identification with Jehovah, in so far as the promised Deliverer, the seed of the woman, was to come through him. "Blessed be Jehovah, the God of Shem" (Gen. 9. 26). Later this promise was narrowed down to Abraham (Gen. 22. 18), renewed to Isaac (Gen. 26. 3, 4), and confirmed to Jacob (Gen. 28. 4).

But when Jacob's twelve sons were about to become twelve tribes, it became necessary to indicate further through which of the tribes the promised seed would appear. Gen. 49. 10 makes it clear that the Messiah should be a descendant of Judah. This prediction is, therefore, in proper sequence of the earlier promises, and is itself followed by the later prophecies that the Messiah is to be of the family of David (1 Chron. 17. 11-14; Jer. 23. 5, 6).

The expression "law-giver," Heb., *mechokek* comes from the root *chakak*, to cut into, to engrave, as was done in the early writing. In Job 19. 23 it is translated *printed* in a book, but better, as the Revised Version has it, *inscribed* in a book. It evidently refers to those who inscribe and make laws, viz., the ancient *sopherim*—scribes and Sanhedrim, as the Chaldiac Targum well paraphrases it. This council of seventy elders is traced by the Rabbis to the days of Moses, and they continued in Judah till Christ came, which was not the case with the other tribes.

The Sanhedrim wielded great political and ecclesiastical power during the time of the second Temple; they were the law-givers of the people.

As a political body the Sanhedrim was dissolved at the destruction of Jerusalem by Titus, but as a religious body it continued at Tiberias, Jabneh, or Jamnia.

A Vision of Peace and Prosperity.

The patriarch's vision pierces the remote ages of the future, and he beholds his great Son enthroned in power, and the peoples (plural in Hebrew) obeying His behests.

"Binding his foal unto the vine (*gephen*),
And his ass's colt unto the choice vine (*sorek*) ;
He washes his garments in wine,
And his vesture in the blood of grapes. "

So common will these trees be that men will tie their animals to them, and so prolific will they be in fruit, that the wine produced from them will be as easy to obtain as the water in which people wash their garments.

"His eyes will be redder than wine,
And his teeth whiter than milk. "

The brightness of the eyes and the whiteness of the teeth will be indications of good, buoyant health.

After predicting the advent of Shiloh—the Rest-giver—there follows in verses 11 and 12, a lovely picture of peace and prosperity. The wayfaring man tying his animal to the branches of the luxuriant vine, while he himself rests quietly under its shade and partakes freely of its luscious fruit that grows in abundance.

A Prayer for the Coming of the Messiah.

The blessing of Moses upon Judah is strikingly in harmony with that of Jacob.

"Hear, O Jehovah, the voice of Judah,
And bring him unto his people,
His hands shall be great (mighty) for him,
And Thou shalt be a help against his adversaries"
(Deut. 33. 7).

"Hear, O Jehovah, the voice of Judah. "

It is the voice of praise and prayer, surely, of the godly of that tribe, many of whom have prayed fervently and often.

It was in the Temple of Jerusalem, the chief city of this tribe that the voice of Judah was often heard, from the prayer of Solomon at its dedication to the petition of the publican, who prayed, "God be merciful to me a sinner."

The many prayers in the book of Psalms written by David, are the voice of Judah that God heard; Solomon's supplication in the Temple, the petitions of Asa, Jehoshaphat, and Hezekiah, who were all of that tribe, were all included in the voice of Judah. The intercessions of Daniel and Nehemiah were also the voice of Judah that God heard and answered. Does not this encourage us also to approach God with our petitions? (Psa. 65. 2).

Finally, this prophetic utterance—as so many others—finds its exhaustive fulfilment in Christ, Judah's greatest representative. He offered up prayers and supplications . . . and was heard. He was able to look up to His Father's face and say, "Father, I thank Thee that Thou hast heard Me, and I know that Thou hearest Me always" (Heb. 5. 7; John 11. 41, 42).

And what a comfort it is to know that as our High Priest intercedes for us in the Heavenly sanctuary, pleading on our behalf the merits of His spotless life and the efficacy of His precious death, His Father will never say nay to Him!

This prophecy having been uttered so long after Judah's death, cannot refer to him personally, and those who only see the tribe of Judah in this verse find it difficult to explain the expression, "And bring him to his people." It surely takes us back to Gen. 49. 10 that predicts Messiah's coming and makes it a landmark in Judah's history. It was to His people that Shiloh primarily came, though alas, they did not receive Him (John. 1. 11).

The pious in Judah, being ignorant of Messiah's advent, continue to pray regularly three times a day for His appearing, "O cause speedily the Sprout (branch) of David, Thy servant, to sprout forth, and exalt His horn in Thy salvation, because we wait for Thy salvation all the day." (Prayer of the eighteen blessings). Similarly in the thirteen articles of his creed the Jew says every morning, "I believe with a perfect faith in the coming of the Messiah, and though He tarries, yet will I wait for Him every day till He come." And O, what grace, that notwithstanding the fact that Judah rejected Him when He first came, when He returns in the clouds of Heaven, "with power and great glory," and His feet will stand upon the Mount of Olives, it will be to save and bless that very people. His hands will truly be mighty (*rav*) for Him, and He will be a help against their enemies, overthrowing the confederacy of nations under the Antichrist and setting His people free.

Of Benaiah, the son of Jehoiada, it is said that he was (*rav pealim*) of mighty deeds. This is true, in a higher sense, of our Lord; *yadav rav lo*, "His hands are great (mighty) for Him." Isa. 63. 1-3 also describes Him as *rav lehoshe-a*, "mighty to save."

"Who art Thou red in Thine apparel, and Thy
garments like him that treadeth in the winefat?
I have trodden the wine-press alone, and of the
people there was none with Me, and I will tread
them in Mine anger and trample them in My
fury" (Isa. 63, 23).

From Rev. 19. 13, 15, we learn that this will be
fulfilled by the Lord Jesus when He comes back from
the opened Heaven, crowned with the many diadems
to subdue the nations, and rule in righteousness.
The kingdoms of this world will then become
the Kingdom of our Lord and of His Christ, and He
shall reign for ever and ever.

The Coming of the Messiah

" MESSIAH'S coming and the tidings are rolling wide and far,
As light flows out in gladness from yon fair morning star.
He is Coming ! and the tidings sweep through the willing air,
With hope that ends for ever time's ages of despair.
This old earth from dreams and slumbers wakes up and says
    Amen,
Land and ocean bid Him welcome, flood and forest join the
    strain.

He is Coming ! and the mountains of Judea ring again,
Jerusalem awakens, and shouts her glad Amen.
He is Coming ! wastes of Horeb, awaken and rejoice :
Hills of Moab, cliffs of Edom, lift the long silent voice.
He is Coming ! sea of Sodom, to heal thy leprous brine,
To give back palm and myrtle, the olive and the vine.

He is Coming ! blighted Carmel, to restore thine olive bowers :
He is Coming ! faded Sharon, to give thee back thy flowers :
Sons of Gentile-trodden Judah, awake ! behold He comes !
Landless and kingless exiles, re-seek your long lost homes :
Back to your ancient valleys, which your fathers loved so well,
In their now crumbled cities, let their children's children dwell.

Drink the last drop of wormwood, from your nation's bitter
    cup,
The bitterest, but the latest, make haste and drink it up :
For He, thy true Messiah, thine own anointed King,
He comes in love and glory, thee endless joy to bring,
Yes, He thy King is Coming, to end thy woes and wrongs,
To give thee joy for mourning, to turn thy sighs to songs.''

CHAPTER VII

Zebulun—Dwelling

" Zebulun shall dwell at the haven of the seas,
And he shall be for an haven of ships,
And his side shall be unto Zidon "   (Gen. 49. 13).

" And of Zebulun he said :
Rejoice, Zebulun, in thy going out ;
And, Issachar, in thy tents,
They shall call the peoples unto the mountain ;
There shall they offer sacrifices of righteousness ;
For they shall suck the abundance of the seas,
And the hidden treasures of the sand "
                                        (Deut. 33. 18, 19).

CHAPTER VII

Zebulun—Dwelling

WHEN Leah gave birth to her sixth son she felt that God had given her a great gift. All these sons would bind her husband's affection to her and he would continue to dwell with her, so she called the name of her son Zebulun—habitation (Gen. 30. 20). Jacob's prediction concerning Zebulun takes us back to this expression at his birth, for though a different word is used in the original for dwelling, the meaning is the same.

"Zebulun shall dwell at the haven of the seas,
    And he shall give shelter to ships. "

It is somewhat difficult to determine Zebulun's exact boundaries, but Jacob's prediction certainly implies that his territory should reach to the seas. Josephus, the Jewish historian of the first century A.D., confirms this. He says: "The tribe of Zebulun's lot included the land which lay as far as Gennesaret, and that which belonged to Carmel and the sea" (Ant. 5. 1, 22).

The Targum also understood it thus. It paraphrases verse 13, "Zebulun shall be on the coasts of the sea, and he shall control the havens; he shall subdue the provinces of the sea with his ships, and his side be unto Zidon. "

How often must Zebulun have given shelter to the storm-tossed ships of the Lake of Galilee, on which were the apostles and our Lord Himself!

Zebulun—a habitation, * was the dwelling place of the prophet Jonah, who lived at Gath-Hepher. It was the home of several of the apostles, Philip, Andrew, Peter, probably also of James, John, and Nathaniel. Above all, it was the dwelling place of our Lord. His blessed feet trod the district more than any other place. It was there He attracted such crowds of people, who gladly listened to His loving, living, burning words, and where they witnessed so many of His mighty works.

It was to His home at Nazareth, in Zebulun, that the Lord Jesus took the two disciples who came to Him and asked, "Rabbi, where dwellest Thou?" It was in Galilee that He appointed His disciples to meet Him after His resurrection. Many of the beautiful parables and illustrations were drawn from Nature round about Him in Galilee, as the seed falling on the hard ground, the stony places, the thorny ground and the good soil, also the drag net and fishes, etc. It was always His way to take the common things around Him and to impart new meaning and life to them, teaching spiritual lessons from material objects.

True to fact, Isaiah prophesied that in the land of Zebulun and Naphtali—the Galilee of the Gentiles—should arise the Divine luminary and shed lustre over that benighted district.

"The people that walk in darkness have seen a great light; they that dwell in the land of the shadow of death, upon them hath the light shined" (Isa. 9. 1, 2; Matt. 4. 14-16).

Then to explain the symbolic language the prophet announces in plain words:

*Zebhul, a habitation is used of the Temple. Solomon said he built the Lord "a house to dwell in" (1 Kings 8. 13). It is used of the Heavens as God's habitation (Isa. 63. 15). Also of the sky as the habitation of the sun and moon (Hab. 3. 11). Sheol is spoken of as the dwelling place, Zebhul, of the dead (Psa. 49. 14).

"Unto us a child is born, unto us a son is given; and the government shall be upon His shoulder, and His Name shall be called, Wonderful, Counsellor, Mighty God, Father of Eternity, Prince of Peace" (Isa. 9. 6).

The Child born, and Son given, Who is at the same time, the Mighty God, and Father of Eternity, is the great light to arise in the land of Zebulun and Naphtali.

A striking fact about this prophecy is that the Land of Zebulun and Naphtali is called the Galilee of the Gentiles, a name more applicable to it in the days of Christ than at the time of the prediction. In the days of our Lord, a great many of the inhabitants of Galilee were Gentiles, Greek mercenaries, and Roman colonists. So that to the prophet was given a vision of the actual conditions of the place as they were at the time the prophecy was to be fulfilled.

In the blessing of Moses (Deut. 33. 18, 19), Zebulun is linked with Issachar.

"Rejoice, Zebulun, at thy going forth, and Issachar in thy tents, nations will they invite to the mountain; there shall they offer sacrifices of righteousness, for they shall suck the abundance of the seas, and the hidden treasures of the sand. "

Zebulun and Issachar were both bidden to rejoice, the one being on the sea-coast, and having the greater opportunities, was to rejoice in his going out, the other being placed on the land, was also to rejoice in abiding in his tents. Zebulun was evidently the more aggressive, while Issachar was more satisfied to continue his agricultural pursuit where he was placed. The Lord knew for what each of them was suited, and He appointed them different positions according to their fitness. Both were to rejoice because they were in the will of God, and in the position where He placed them. It was also a joy in witness bearing.

Our service for God may lie in different spheres, and among different people, but fitted and equipped by God, let us joyfully exclaim, "Here am I, send me" and use me. Remembering at the same time, that the place of greater privilege is the place of greater responsibility.

Does Moses, "the man of God," envisage here the apostles of these tribes going forth joyously from Galilee with the glad tidings of salvation, calling the Gentiles to worship God, as it were, upon the mountain?

"Nations shall they invite to the mountain;
   There shall they offer sacrifices of righteousness."

To what mountain does Moses refer here? It can only be Mount Moriah, where the Temple stood, as it is here connected with the offering of sacrifices. Moses gives no name to the mountain, and this is what he does right through the book of Deuteronomy, where he refers to the Temple, without saying where it was to be situated, but only as *the place* (*Hammakom*) that the Lord will choose.

In 2 Chron. 3. 1, the inspired writer brings together in one verse a number of Scriptures that reveal God's purpose regarding the mountain.

"Then Solomon began to build the House of Jehovah at Jerusalem, on Mount Moriah, where Jehovah appeared unto David, his father, which he made ready in the place that David had appointed in the threshing floor of Ornan the Jebusite."

This first step takes us back to Gen. 22, where we read that Abraham was sent up all the way from Beersheba, in the extreme south of the promised land, to Mount Moriah to offer up Isaac, his beloved

son, as a burnt offering. It is called one of the mountains (verse 2), Abraham calls it JEHOVAH JIREH;
this is explained, "as it is said unto this day, In the
mount of the Lord it shall be seen (or provided, v. 14).
Four times over it is also spoken of as "The Place"
(*Hammakom*), as in Deuteronomy, "THE PLACE THAT
THE LORD SHALL CHOOSE." In this book it is found 21
times.

David was divinely led to purchase that parcel of
ground from Ornan the Jebusite, in order to erect
an altar and to offer up burnt offerings to God. This
did not happen by chance, indeed we are informed
that it was the angel of Jehovah Who bade Gad,
the Seer, to tell David to do so. And God graciously
indicated His approval by sending down fire from
Heaven to consume the burnt and peace offerings,
and the plague was stayed (1 Chron. 21. 18-21).
This, then, was the place or mountain on which
Solomon built the Temple.

No wonder, therefore, that the people of Zebulun
were bidden to rejoice as their representatives went
forth on their apostolic errand. And thank God for as
many of the nations as had the grace to respond to the
Divine call. We are assured that the time is coming
when all nations shall flow to that mountain.

"And it shall come to pass in the last days that the
mountain of the Lord's house shall be established
on the top of the mountains, and shall be exalted
above the hills; and all nations shall flow unto it
(as the peaceful flow of a river). And many
peoples shall go and say, Come ye, and let us go
up to the mountain of Jehovah, to the house of
the God of Jacob; and He shall teach us of His ways,
and we will walk in His paths; for out of Zion
shall go forth the Law, and the word of Jehovah
from Jerusalem" (Isa. 2. 2, 3).

Israel converted and illumined by the Divine light shining upon them, will become a nation of Missionaries calling the Gentiles to the worship of Jehovah.

"The Gentiles shall come to thy light and kings to the brightness of thy rising" (Isa. 60. 1-3).

We are not told quite as much concerning Zebulun as of some of the other tribes, but they come in for praise from Deborah, because in response to Barak, they followed, in a long train, their military commander against Sisera (that is, they were a great army), as is evidently the meaning of Judges 5. 14. * From verse 18 we learn that together with the tribe of Naphtali "they jeoparded their lives even unto death," in that great cause. They likewise showed readiness to join Gideon in subduing the Midianites.

It is also recorded to their credit, in 1 Chron. 12. 33, that fifty thousand of them who were expert in war, joined in the national acclamation of David as King over all Israel. That was a greater number than any other tribe, and what is still better, they were wholehearted and sincere—"not of a double heart." And though they had to come all the way from Galilee to Hebron, in Judah, they joined with their brethren nearer at hand in bringing on asses and camels, on mules and on oxen, bread, meal-food, cakes of figs, bunches of raisins, wine and oil, oxen and sheep, abundantly, "for there was joy in Israel." What a lovely picture this is of the time when the greater David will be crowned by all Israel as their King and Lord!

Some of the Zebulunites accepted Hezekiah's invi-

---

*In the Authorised Version it is rendered, "They that handle the pen of the writer." In the Revised, "They that handle the marshal's staff." In the Hebrew only three words are used for it, *moshechim beshebhet sopher*. Moshechim means "that draw out" as a long army. In Judges 4. 6 it is translated "draw" in connection with the army. *Shebet* means a staff, not pen. *Sopher*, "writer" or "numberer" is used for the field marshal in 2 Kings 25. 19, 2 Chron. 26. 11, and Jer. 52. 25, because it was his duty to number or marshal the army.

tation to join Judah in their great celebration of the Passover at Jerusalem (2 Chron. 30. 11).

Moses, like Jacob, places Zebulun by the seas, he does more, he promises them that, "They shall suck of the abundance of the seas and of the treasures hid in the sand." This has in measure already been verified to them. For many centuries, however, they have been exiled from their land, and even at present they do not enjoy these blessings, but it is very remarkable that Ezekiel, in replacing the tribes in the promised land, fixes Zebulun's boundaries in the extreme south, the last portion but one in a strip of territory which, as a careful study will show, must run from the Mediterranean on the West to the Dead Sea on the East; so that the great wealth that has recently been discovered to be in the Dead Sea will fall in Zebulun's portion, thus fulfilling, as never before, the promise, "they shall suck of the abundance of the seas and the treasures hid in the sand."

On careful study we are persuaded that the blessings of the Millennium cannot be left out from the purview of these prophecies that deal with the history of Israel, and this is surely indicated by Jacob when, in calling together his sons, he said: "Gather yourselves together, that I may tell you that which shall befall you in the last days" (*acharith hayyamim*). In the purposes of God the whole history of mankind points on, and leads up to, the age when our Lord shall sit enthroned and rule the world in righteousness and peace, when "Jehovah shall be King over the whole earth; in that day shall Jehovah be one and His Name one" (Zech. 14. 9).

The Glory of Zebulun

WHILE faithful to thy covenant King,
  In holy might excelling,
Thy haven welcomed storm-tossed ships,
  Home to thy quiet dwelling.

Thy thousands scattered Jabin's pride,
  In Kishon's stormy fight ;
Thy tens of thousands swept away
  The conquering Amorite.

And when the tribes to Salem poured
  Their festal tides along,
Thy banner on the hill of God
  Waved with the jubilant song.

O Zebulun, thy valleys spread,
  Fair in the morning's sheen ;
But fairest when *He* dwelt in thee,
  The sinless Nazarene.

Great was thy glory when thou dwell'st
  At haven of the sea ;
But greatest when He sheltered souls
  On thy shore, blue Galilee.

And even now in Cana's name,
  In Nazareth and its hill,
In Magdala, on Tabor's height,
  A fragrance lingers still ;

Which shall yet fill the dewy air,
  Of that long-looked-for day,
When He returns Who was thy Light,
  Returns to shine for aye.

PAULIN.

Chapter VIII

Issachar—Reward

" Issachar is a strong ass,
Couching between the sheepfolds.
And he saw that the rest was good,
And that the land was pleasant,
So he inclined his shoulder to bear ;
And became a worker unto tribute " (Gen. 49. 14, 15).

" Rejoice, Zebulun, in thy going forth,
And Issachar in thy tents,
Nations will they invite to the mountain ;
There shall they offer sacrifices of righteousness,
For they shall suck the abundance of the seas,
And the hidden treasures of the sand "

(Deut. 33. 18, 19).

CHAPTER VIII

Issachar—Reward

NO stress is laid here directly on the meaning of Issachar, as in the case of most of the other tribes, but in its signification the name expresses a great truth. *Sachar* means, "to hire for payment," hence "reward."

This was evidently the thought in Leah's mind when she gave birth to her fifth son, whom she called Issachar. "God gave me my reward," she said.

Leah had a double reason for giving him this name. (*a*) because he was given her as a reward for the mandrakes, or love-apples that she gave to Rachel (Gen. 30. 16), and (*b*) as compensation for her unselfishness in giving Zilpah to Jacob (ibid. 30. 18). The name stands thus as a witness to Divine retribution as taught throughout the Bible.

The Lesson the Name Issachar Teaches.

In its Hebrew spelling we find the name *Yeshsachar* in Jer. 31 16, where it is translated, "There is a reward."

Again, "Be ye strong, therefore, and let not your hands be weak; for there is a reward (*yesh sachar*) for your work," were the Spirit-indited words of Azariah, the son of Oded, to Asa, and the people of Judah, as he sought to encourage them in their effort of reformation (2 Chron. 15. 7).

This was recognised by the apostle as a Divine principle, "He that cometh to God must believe that He is, and that He is a rewarder of them that diligently seek Him" (Heb. 11. 6). In another place, the same apostle writes: "God is not unrighteous to forget your work and labour of love, which ye have showed towards His Name" (Heb. 6. 10).

Christ the Rewarder.

"Behold," cries the prophet, "Jehovah hath proclaimed unto the end of the world, say ye to the daughter of Zion, Behold thy Salvation cometh; behold His reward is with Him and His work before Him" (Isa. 62. 11). Salvation not as an abstract idea merely, but a person with a reward to bestow and a work to accomplish.

In harmony with this verse the Lord Jesus assured His disciples:

"The Son of Man shall come in the glory of the Father, with His angels, and then He shall reward every man according to his works" (Matt. 16. 27).

Also in His resurrection power and glory He sealed the visions of the Apocalypse in Patmos, with these words, "Behold I come quickly, and My reward is with Me to give every man according as his work shall be" (Rev. 22. 12). Our Lord is the Salvation, Who also gives the reward.

Salvation and Reward.

This, of course, does not contradict the doctrine of grace. So far as our salvation is concerned we rest entirely upon the finished work of Christ. Nothing that we can do will save us, "By grace are ye saved, through faith; and that not of yourselves, it is the gift of God" (Eph. 2. 8).

But forgiveness of sins is not all that our God has for His children, He has something much better and more glorious. "Whom He justified, them He also glorified." Truly in His presence is fulness of joy; at His right hand there are pleasures for evermore (Psa. 16. 11). "Eye hath not seen, nor ear heard, neither have entered into the heart of man, the things which God hath prepared for them that love Him" (1 Cor. 2. 9).

Salvation from sin is the portal, but only the portal, through which we enter into a more blessed and glorious life and experience. Beyond mere salvation our Saviour will give rewards to those whose works, like gold, silver, precious stones, will stand the test of fire. "If any man's work will abide which he hath built thereupon (i.e., upon Christ as the foundation), he shall receive a reward" (1 Cor. 3. 14).

Four Crowns as Rewards.

In figurative language the apostle speaks of the rewards as crowns. There are, for instance; (a) The Crown of Life for fidelity to God in temptation and suffering (Jas. 1. 12; Rev. 2. 10). (b) The Crown of Righteousness for fidelity in service, as Paul who could say, "I have fought a good fight, I have finished my course, I have kept the faith" (2 Tim. 4. 7, 8). (c) The Crown of Rejoicing for fidelity in winning souls (1 Thess. 2. 19). (d) The Crown of Glory, for fidelity in shepherding the flock (1 Peter 5. 2-4).

These are not fading laurel wreaths with which the successful winners in the race and the victorious combatants in the arena were crowned. "They do it," says the apostle, "to obtain a corruptible crown but we an incorruptible" (1 Cor. 9. 25).

Happy is the man who will one day be privileged to hear the blessed words falling from the Master's lips: "Well done, thou good and faithful servant;

thou hast been faithful over a few things, I will make thee ruler over many things; enter thou into the joy of thy Lord" (Matt. 25. 21).

Does Moses in Deut. 33, describe Issachar's reward, when he bids him rejoice in his tents, and promises him that he will suck of the abundance of the seas, or perhaps what refers more to him, the treasures hid in the sand?

Issachar a Landowner.

Moses links Zebulun and Issachar together, but is in complete harmony with Jacob about them. Jacob depicts Issachar as couching between the sheepfolds, enjoying a comfortable rest and a pleasant land; Moses speaks of him as rejoicing in his tents. Genesis makes Zebulun a maritime people, having to do with ships and a harbour, and Issachar with agriculture, as a successful worker in the ground; Deuteronomy also connects them both with the sea and the sand.

Issachar is compared to a strong-boned ass. In our western lands, the ass is a despised animal, but not so in the East where it is looked upon as a useful, patient, and hardy animal. There is, therefore, nothing derogatory to Issachar in this comparison, it rather ascribes to him, patience, endurance, and a capacity for work.

The word *mishpethaim*, translated in the Authorised Version "two burdens," has been referred by some to the panniers, or baskets, placed on the sides of the ass, as a receptacle for the baggage it carried; but "sheepfolds," as in the Revised Version is a better rendering, as it describes the resting of the farmer-shepherd among his sheep, very applicable to the tribe of Issachar. This form of the word is only found once elsewhere (Judges 5. 16), and there it evidently has the meaning of sheepfold, and is thus translated.

Josephus says that Issachar's portion of land extended in length from Mount Carmel to the River Jordan, and in breadth to Mount Tabor. This comprises most of the plain of Esdraelon, a very fertile piece of land. The Rabbis compare Bethshean to the gate of Paradise. The writer, who had the privilege of visiting that district two years ago, was greatly impressed with the beauty and fertility of it, especially at Jenin—the ancient En Gannim.

The expression, "a servant," or better, "a worker unto tribute," is specially applied to Issachar, because his portion of the land was very fertile and produced much to supply the king with his required provision, which in the case of Solomon was very large.

Solomon was able to give Hiram, king of Tyre, 20,000 measures of pure oil (1 Kings 5. 11). The Hebrew word *mas* here translated "tribute," does not necessarily mean a gift to a foreign power, it is also used for a contribution to one's own ruler (see 1 Kings 5. 13, where the same word is translated "levy" that was raised by Solomon from Israel).

Jehoshaphat, the son of Paruah of Issachar, was one of the commissariat officers providing for the king's household (1 Kings 4. 17). The fertile districts of Taanach and Megiddo, which also provided for King Solomon's needs (ibid. 4. 12), though ceded to Manasseh were really in the country of Issachar (Joshua 17. 11).

Issachar's Role Among the Tribes.

On the journey through the wilderness, Issachar marched foremost with Judah and Zebulun, making the strongest triplet. On leaving Egypt, Issachar was 54,400 strong, and while some of the tribes decreased in numbers during the wilderness journey, Issachar increased by 9,900 men, and numbered at the second census 64,300 (Num. 26. 25).

In the battle against Sisera this tribe earned Deborah's praise as some of those who came to the help of the Lord against the mighty.

On David's accession to the throne, Issachar supplied 87,000 warriors for his army (1 Chron. 7. 5). In those days they must have had a good deal of influence amongst the other tribes, for in 1 Chron. 12. 32, we are told that they were "men that had understanding of the times, to know what Israel ought to do." Good would it have been for the spiritual and national welfare of the Jews in the days of Christ, if they had had an understanding of the times to know what Israel ought to do, but, alas! our Lord had to rebuke them because they knew how to discern the face of the heavens, but could not discern the signs of the times (Matt. 16. 3). On another occasion, the Lord Jesus weeping over Jerusalem, declared, "If thou hadst known, even thou at least in this thy day, the things that belong to thy peace; but now they are hid from thine eyes" (Luke 19. 42).

The Importance of the Times.

How many there are to-day who do not realise the importance of the times in which we live! We need to read our newspapers with the open Bible before us, and see how wonderfully all that is happening in the world to-day is in complete harmony with the predictions of God's purposes in the Scriptures of truth.

Did not the Lord Jesus give us a number of signs revealing His plan for the ages, and heralding His approach? "Behold the fig tree and all the trees; When they shoot forth, ye see and know of your own selves that summer is now nigh at hand. So likewise

ye, when ye see these things come to pass, know ye
that the Kingdom of God is nigh at hand" (Luke
21. 29-31).

One of the judges who defended Israel was a man
of Issachar, named Tola, the son of Puah; he ruled
23 years; later on, Baasha, a man of this tribe, was
the instrument of carrying out the sentence of punishment against the house of Jeroboam, pronounced by
Ahijah the Shilonite, and became king in his place.

Baasha reigned 24 years, but alas! he walked in
the footsteps of Jeroboam, whose household he was
the instrument of destroying. He did not learn the
lesson which Jeroboam's end should have taught
him. He continued the worship of the calves, so
that to him was meted out a similar punishment.
His son, Elah, was killed by his servant, Zimri,
after a short reign of two years, and his entire household was slain, according to the prophecy of Jehu,
the son of Hanani (1 Kings 16. 1-13).

Issachar, a Battle Ground.

Issachar's portion of land, being an extensive
plain where large armies could easily manœuvre,
formed the chief battle ground of Palestine.

There Barak with only 10,000 men discomfited
Sisera's hosts with their 900 iron chariots, and thus
called forth Deborah's historic song of praise (Jud. 5).

There Gideon delivered Israel from the Midianites
and Amalekites (Judges 6. 12-25).

There, too, on the slopes of Gilboa, the Israelites
met with the terrible catastrophe when they were
defeated by the Philistines; Saul falling upon his
sword, and his three sons being slain (1 Sam. 31.
1-6). There, also, good King Josiah was slain by
Pharaoh-Necho, causing the great national lam-
entation (2 Chron. 35. 23-25).

This important battle ground, and all the wars carried on there, foreshadowed Armageddon, the decisive and final battle of this age, when our Lord, on His return, will destroy the anti-Christian army who will gather there (Rev. 16. 16). Armageddon is simply the Greek pronunciation of the Hebrew *Har-Megiddon*—the hill of Megiddo or Megiddon, the ancient town on the plain of Jezreel, close to Mount Carmel which Solomon fortified. It is also called the vale of Megiddo and represents the whole district.

A Scene on Carmel.

It was on that side of Carmel overlooking the land of Issachar, that Elijah called together King Ahab and the people of Israel, with their 850 false prophets, and by his indomitable courage and faithful testimony to the Lord, was made the instrument of bringing Israel back to God, as in answer to his prayer fire fell from Heaven and consumed the sacrifice on the altar, the wood and the stones, and licked up the water in the trench, so that when the people saw it they fell upon their faces, and cried, "JEHOVAH, HE IS THE ELOHIM; JEHOVAH, HE IS THE ELOHIM."

This incident will surely have its counterpart, when, at the Coming of our Lord, through the witness of Elijah, Israel will be reconciled unto Him, and will be brought back into covenant relationship with Jehovah, and the heart of the fathers, together with the heart of the children, shall turn to Him* (Psa. 118. 27, 28; Mal. 4. 5, 6).

Elisha and the Shunammite.

Another important incident in Issachar is that connected with the prophet Elisha, and the "great

---

*This is the force of the original. The Hebrew preposition *al* translated "upon" in Mal. 4. 6, should be rendered "along with." In Exodus 35. 22 *al* is translated "both and."

woman" of Shunem, who showed kindness to the prophet by giving him hospitality, and by setting apart a room for his use. As a reward for this a son was given to her.

When the boy, several years later, fell ill and died his mother at once ran for help to the prophet, who was made God's instrument to restore the child to life again.

The Lord Jesus at Nain.

This reminds us of another touching incident of a similar nature that took place in the days of our Lord near the same spot. The scene comes before us. In the city of Nain, a Jewish funeral procession wends its way, a young man has died and is being carried to the grave on a bier. His poor, broken-hearted mother, now bereft of her only son, follows falteringly, weeping. Then the Lord Jesus comes near, and being moved with compassion for the sorrowing mother, speaks words of comfort to her. He touches the bier, the procession, wondering what will happen, stands still. Then the Lord Jesus addresses the corpse, "Young man, I say unto thee, Arise. " And he that was dead sits up and begins to speak, and, to his mother's great joy, is delivered to her alive and well. The people marvel, and glorify God, saying, "A great Prophet is risen up among us, God hath visited His people" (Luke 7. 11-16).

A glance at the map will show that Nain was quite near to the old township of Shunem, where Elisha, whose name means "God is Saviour," prefiguring the Lord Jesus, brought the lad of Issachar from the dead to life again, but the act of Christ at the gate of Nain is, in itself, a pledge and a prophecy that "the hour is coming when the dead shall hear the voice of the Son of God; and they that hear shall live" (John 5. 25).

Issachar and Zebulun, Leah's fifth and sixth sons, are coupled together in the blessing of Moses. They travelled together in the wilderness journey; were mentioned together with approval in Deborah's song; were neighbours in the land as divided by Joshua. Ezekiel also places Issachar next to Zebulun in the fresh division of the land for the Millennium, and in the inscription of their names on the gates of the new city (Ezek. 48. 25, 33).

Issachar and Jezreel

WHERE bloomed in pride of beauty fair Jezreel,
There Issachar's majestic strength was spread.
The burden bearer of the common weal,
He bent between the loads his patient head,
Bearing the Assyrian yoke when Egypt fled,
And Egypt's when the Assyrian curb was broken.
Thy plain was watered oft with blood and tears ;
Grief for Megiddo's slain is still the token
Of future wail when time's allotted years
Have run their chequered course, and Zion's King appears.

Blest be thy portion, Issachar ! for One
Has trod thy plains Who came the world to save.
But thou in lands afar a tent and a grave
For sins of dark idolatry has found.
Till, taught by Heaven to make the better choice,
No home is thine.   Yet soon a thrilling sound
Mine ear shall hear, a death awakening voice
Shall bid thee once again within thy tents rejoice.

Then sighs of deeper grief the air shall fill
Than Hadadrimmon's mourning, for the Cross
Seen in salvation's light all hearts shall thrill.
That sight shall change all glory into dross.
The Prince of Peace proclaims the jubilee !
The Day of Coming time shall that of Jezreel be ! "
                                        PAULIN.

CHAPTER IX

Dan—Judge

" Dan shall judge his people,
As one of the tribes of Israel.
Dan shall be a serpent in the way,
A horned serpent in the path,
That biteth the horse's heels,
So that its rider falleth backward.
I have waited for Thy Salvation, O Jehovah."

(Gen. 49. 16-18).

" And of Dan he said,
Dan is a lion's whelp,
That leapeth forth from Bashan "

(Deut. 33. 22).

CHAPTER IX

Dan—Judge

The Name of Dan

JACOB puts similar play upon the name of Dan as did Rachel at his birth. She felt that God had judged her favourably, answered her prayer and, through her maid Bilhah, had given her a son, whom she received to her heart as her own, and called his name Dan—"Judge." This is not, of course, in harmony with the higher standard of Christ in the New Testament, but God in His grace overruled it.

Jacob makes Dan's name a prophecy of the future of the tribe (*Dan yadin ammo*). "The judge shall judge his people as one of the tribes of Israel." As Dan was the first son borne to him of the bondwoman, the Patriarch, by this declaration concerning him, gives him a place with equal rights among the sons borne by Rachel and Leah; while prophetically he appoints him a position in restored Israel. Dan fell early into idolatry, and for some time was little heard of; yet, at the end he is predicted to play a part among the other tribes of the nation.

Dan commenced well. He, apparently, had only one son, named Hushim, when the family left Canaan (Gen. 46. 23), but the tribe increased very rapidly, so that at the Exodus from Egypt the males of Dan over 20 years of age, numbered 62,700, next in strength to Judah, and during the wilderness journey they further increased to 64,400.

Their position while travelling in the wilderness, was to the north of the Tabernacle, and they formed the chief tribe of the three bringing up the rear, having Asher on the one side, and Napthali on the other.

On their tribal standard, according to tradition, they had emblazoned an eagle, changed from a serpent, in harmony with one of the faces of the Cherubim.

Scripture often speaks of fierce and destructive enemies under the figure of serpents. Jeremiah, referring to Israel's enemies coming from the direction of Dan, likens them to serpents and basilisks, who will not be charmed, *i.e.*, will not be dissuaded or hindered from their work of destruction, but as he speaks of Dan he recalls his characteristic as given to him by Jacob (Jer. 8. 16, 17). Dan, when in communion with God, was a dangerous foe to en-counter, but in his state of apostasy, others were made, like serpents, dangerous to him.

A Remarkable Theophany.

Samson, who was a Danite, judged Israel twenty years. His parents were godly, praying people (see Judges 13. 8), to whom the Angel of Jehovah con-descendingly appeared and foretold the birth of the child. As to who this angel was, we get a clue from Judges 13. 18, where we learn that His Name is Wonderful (*Pele*), the same as in Isaiah 9. 6, where it is distinctly a title of Christ. As was His Name, so were His acts, for in verse 19 we are told that "He did wondrously," while He would not partake of any food Manoah offered Him, He approved of a burnt offering, and as the flame of the sacrifice rose heaven-ward the Angel of Jehovah ascended with it, while Manoah and his wife looked on in wonderment.

What a picture this is of the Lord Jesus identifying Himself with the offering that typified His acceptance with the Father! Truly in more than one sense did He act wondrously.

It was at Ajalon, in the tribe of Dan, that God's gracious interposition on behalf of His people took place, when, in answer to Joshua's prayer, the day was prolonged to enable the Israelites to obtain a decisive victory over the combined forces of the Canaanite nations. Ajalon, in Dan, was afterwards assigned to the Levites.

Dan's Lapse into Idolatry.

Dan's territory lay between that of Judah on the south, Ephraim and Benjamin on the east, with part of their western boundary at Joppa by the sea. But this piece of land was quite small. The tribe was also hard pressed by the Amorites, and afterwards by the Philistines, for they failed to cast out their enemies as God intended them to do, and finding the land insufficient a number of them went to the north of Palestine, conquered the inhabitants of Leshem, or Laish, as it was called, and settled there, calling the place Dan.

When Jeroboam, the son of Nebat, began to reign over the ten tribes, he made that city one of the centres of calf worship; that being the northern extremity of his kingdom, as Bethel was the southern (1 Kings 12. 28-30). Jeroboam was not likely to meet with any resistance to his scheme from the Danites, as they themselves were similarly inclined.

Judges 18 gives an account of the 600 Danites, who, on their establishing themselves at Laish, set up image worship, having Jonathan, the son of Gershom, the son of Manasseh (or better, the son of Moses, as the Revised Version has it), for their priest.

The ancient city of Dan is now identified with Tel el Kady, one of the sources of the Jordan.

Jacob likens Dan to a serpent by the way, and as a horned serpent in the path, that biteth the horse's heels so that its rider falls backwards.

The Hebrew, *Shephiphon*, is generally understood to be the cerastes—a vicious serpent with two little horns on its head, that hides in the sand or in some crevice of the path, and suddenly attacks the passers-by.   Moses likens Dan to a young lion leaping from Bashan.   In both cases the likeness is to an animal suddenly springing on its prey.   This characterised the Danites in their sudden fall upon the inhabitants of Laish; also Samson in his attacks upon the Philistines.

Jacob's Inspired Hope.

The exclamation with which Jacob ends his prophecy concerning Dan is very significant.   "For Thy Salvation have I waited, O Jehovah."   This expresses both man's helplessness and God's deliverance.

Was the Patriarch viewing Dan's lapse into sin and its consequences that made him cast himself thus upon God's mercy?

The Targummim, or the Chaldaic paraphrases, which date back to the days of Christ, very strikingly put it, "Our Father, Jacob, said, Not for the salvation of Gideon, the son of Joash, does my soul look out, for that is only temporary, and not for the salvation of Samson, for that is only transient, but for the salvation promised in Thy Word for Thy people, the sons of Israel; for that salvation does my soul look out" (Jerusalem Targum *in loc*).

Targum Jonathan Ben Uziel also paraphrases it: "Jacob said, when he saw Gideon, the son of Joash; and Samson, the son of Manoah, who were to bring deliverance, Not for the salvation of Gideon do I look, nor for the salvation of Samson do I hope, because their salvation is but for their time; but for Thy Salvation am I looking and hoping, for it is an eternal salvation." Another edition has it, "But for the salvation of Messiah the Son of David, Who will save Israel and deliver them from exile; for that Salvation does my soul wait."

The Lord Jesus is the Salvation hoped for, His name in Hebrew, Joshua, or in full, Jehoshua, means "Jehovah is salvation," and the name describes the Person.

Israel's salvation, national and spiritual, is entirely dependant on Christ and awaits His return. Nationally He will save them from the Antichrist and the confederacy of nations that will so trouble them (Zech. 14. 1-5). Spiritually, too, He is the only means of their salvation:

"And so all Israel shall be saved; as it is written, There shall come out of Sion the Deliverer, and shall turn away ungodliness from Jacob" (Rom. 11. 26).

Depicting the Coming of the Messiah, the prophet puts striking words into the lips of his people:

"Lo, this is our God, we have waited for Him, and He will save us; this is Jehovah, we have waited for Him; we will be glad and rejoice in His salvation" (Isa. 25. 9).

This reads like an inspired commentary on Jacob's expression of hope, and points to Christ in whom it is to be fulfilled.

The pious Jews repeat every morning in the thirteen articles of their creed:

"I believe with perfect faith in the Coming of the Messiah, and although He tarry I will wait for Him every day till He come."

Habakkuk, while looking out on his watch tower,

was given a vision and was commanded to write it
out and make it plain upon tablets, that he may run
who readeth it; for the vision was for an appointed
time, and though it tarry he tells us to wait for it,
because it will surely come and not tarry.

Now this, as it appears from the context, is quoted
in Heb. 10. 37, 38, and is evidently applied to the
return of Christ.

"For yet a very little while,
And He that cometh shall come
And shall not tarry."

The Hebrew pronoun *Lo*, translated "it," is really
masculine, and also means "Him," as it is translated in the Epistle to the Hebrews.   Truly, our hope
is the Lord Jesus Christ.

It is no use looking to any human source for help
and deliverance:

"Not by the might of an army (or multitude) nor
by the power of the individual, but by My Spirit,
saith Jehovah of Hosts" (Zech. 4. 6).

For physical mercies and spiritual blessings, God
is the true source.   "Truly, vain is the help of
man."

"I will lift up mine eyes unto the mountains;
Whence shall my help come?
My help cometh from Jehovah;
The Maker of Heaven and earth" (Psa. 121.
1, 2).

Salvation is God's gracious provision for us; nothing
that we can do for ourselves, and nothing that other
people can do for us will bring us salvation.   It is by
the efficacy of the death of Christ that we are saved,
and by the merits of His spotless life that we are
justified, and we exclaim with Jacob of old,

"FOR THY SALVATION HAVE I WAITED, O
JEHOVAH."

Dan's Eventual Restoration.

In full agreement with this expression of hope, we are assured of Dan's final restoration in the Scriptures of truth, for while their name is left out in Rev. 7 from among the tribes that are sealed for protection from earthly suffering, Ezekiel gives them a permanent position amongst the other tribes in the restored land, placing them in the most northerly portion of it (Ezek. 48. 1).

Dan's name is also inscribed upon one of the twelve gates of the Holy City, by the side of Joseph and Benjamin (Ezek. 48. 32).

What marvellous grace is here displayed before us by our God! In spite of their sin and rebellion, in spite of their apostasy and idolatry, God's love will reach even to them, and His covenant with Abraham, Isaac, and Jacob, and His promises through Moses and the Prophets, can never fail for any of the tribes of Israel. There is efficacy in the precious blood of Christ to cleanse every penitent who seeks His salvation. And when God pours upon that people the spirit of grace and supplication, and they look upon Him Whom they have pierced, and mourn, the fountain is opened to them for sin and uncleanness, Jacob's expectation will be fulfilled and "all Israel shall be saved."

Bezaleel's companion in constructing the Tabernacle was Aholiab, the son of Ahisamach, of the tribe of Dan, who, like Bezaleel, was filled with wisdom of heart, to work all manner of workmanship of the engraver, and of the skilful workman, and of the embroiderer in blue, and in purple, in scarlet, and in fine linen, and of the weaver. Huram, the chief skilful workman in building the Temple, was also the son of a Danite woman, who was married to a man of Tyre. He, too, is described as being endued with understanding, "skilful to work in gold, and in silver, in brass, in iron, in stone and in timber, in purple, in blue, and in fine linen, and in crimson, also to grave any manner of graving, and to devise any device" (2 Chron. 2. 13, 14).

Some think that Huram was a proselyte to the Jewish faith, and thus foreshadowed the Gentiles being brought into the commonwealth of Israel, and building up with them the spiritual temple composed of living stones out of all nationalities, of whom the prophet speaks.

"They that are afar off shall come and build in the Temple of Jehovah" (Zech. 6. 15).

It is to this that Paul refers when he writes:

"Now in Christ Jesus ye who were sometimes far off are made nigh by the blood of Christ . . . Now, therefore, ye are no more strangers and foreigners, but fellow-citizens with the saints, and of the household of God, and are built upon the foundation of the apostles and prophets, Jesus Christ Himself being the chief corner stone, in Whom all the building fitly framed together groweth into an holy Temple in the Lord" (Eph. 2. 13, 19-21).

Chapter X

Gad—The Warrior

" Gad, a troop shall overcome him,
But he shall overcome at the last "

(Gen. 49. 19).

" And of Gad, He said,
Blessed be He that enlargeth Gad ;
He dwelleth as a lion,
And teareth the arm with the crown of the head.
And he provideth the first part for himself,
For there was the Lawgiver's portion reserved,
And He came with the heads of the people,
He executeth the righteousness of Jehovah,
And His judgments with Israel "

(Deut. 33. 20, 21).

CHAPTER X

Gad—The Warrior

THE prediction concerning Gad is brief and expressive. It is a play upon the name of the tribe, and in the Hebrew, forms a fourfold alliteration. *Gad gedud yegudennu vehu yagud akev.*

In translating, it is not easy to retain its paronymous form, perhaps the best and most literal rendering of the verse would be, "Crowd, a crowd shall crowd upon Him, but he shall crowd at the rear," or "at the last."

We are taken back to Gen. 30. 10, 11, where we are told that Zilpah, Leah's maid, gave birth to a son, whom her mistress reckoned as her own, and exclaimed, *ba gad*, "a troop cometh"; thus indicating her satisfaction at the number of sons given her, and at the same time expressing her expectation that more would yet come.

Some translate Leah's expression *ba gad* "fortune cometh," but the rendering of the Authorised Version is preferable. The general meaning of the word is, "a band of men," "a crowd." It is translated "army" four times; "band" fourteen times; "company" four times, and "troop" nine times.

The Patriarch takes up the expression used by Leah and applies it to the tribe; his words are a prayer and a prophecy, as is every inspired petition. It predicts the warring character of Gad. Though not so numerous as the other tribes, they were evidently brave men. Their inheritance lay on the east of Jordan, but together with Reuben, and the half tribe of Manasseh, they crossed the river armed, and fought side by side with their brethren and helped them to conquer the land before going back to their own territory. For this they received the commendation and blessing of Joshua (Joshua 22. 1-5).

Gad's Inheritance.

Their portion of land on the east of Jordan was greatly exposed to attacks of marauding bands, who sometimes pressed these tribes hard, and in order to defend themselves they developed a great fighting disposition. In the days of Saul, they, together with the Reubenites and half tribe of Manasseh, made war with the Hagarites whom they conquered, and the inspired chronicler speaks of them as "valiant men, able to bear buckler and sword, and to shoot with bow, and skilful in war" (1 Chron. 5. 18).

It is further said in their praise, that they "cried to God in the battle, and He was entreated of them; because they put their trust in Him." They evidently did not rely upon their prowess and skill in using weapons (1 Chron., 5. 20).

Is not this the secret of every true victory? "There is no king saved by the multitude of an host; a mighty man is not delivered by much strength. A horse is a vain thing for safety, neither shall he deliver by his great strength" (Psa. 33. 16, 17).

Lessons of Gad's Experience.

In the experience of Gad, dark clouds alternated with bright sunshine, first defeat, then victory.

In varying degree this is the lot of most men, but the rest is all the more enjoyable after the struggle. We appreciate things by contrast, the heavy down-pour is as necessary as the sunshine. The rough wind causes the tree to send its roots all the deeper into the ground, and makes it strong; likewise, our struggles and hardships are meant to strengthen our characters, and to enable us the better to endure hardships as good soldiers of the Cross.

It is specially good for us to learn our weakness that we may seek help from Him, Who is MIGHTY TO SAVE, that we may overcome at the last. Truly, "In all these things we are more than conquerors through Him that loved us."

Fidelity of the Tribe.

Later, some of these Gadites gave great support to David while he was yet at Ziklag. Here again they are described as "men of might and men of war, fit for the battle, that could handle shield and buckler, whose faces are like the faces of lions, and were swift as the roes upon the mountains . . . These are they that went over Jordan in the first month, when it had overflown all its banks; and they put to flight all them of the valleys, both toward the east and toward the west" (1 Chron. 12. 8, 15).

This is in complete agreement with Jacob's prophecy concerning this tribe, and it is, surely, recorded to encourage us in our spiritual warfare for Christ. There are many enemies to be subdued, and much land to be possessed. Let us heed the exhortation, "Fight the good fight of faith," and again, "Put on the whole armour of God, that ye may be able to stand against the wiles of the devil. For we wrestle not against flesh and blood, but against principalities, against powers, against the rulers of the darkness of this world, against spiritual wickedness in high places" (Eph. 6. 11, 12). "The weapons of our warfare are not carnal, but mighty through God to the pulling down of strongholds" (2 Cor. 10. 4). For us also there is provided a complete panoply; the girdle of truth, the breastplate of righteousness, the shield of faith, the helmet of salvation, and the sword of the Spirit. With these, fighting under Christ, our great Captain, we shall be more than conquerors.

These warriors and their fellows from the east of Jordan, 120,000 of them, came to make David king, desirous to do him honour, ready to fight his battles. Are we thus loyal to our greater King David?

These Gadites had crossed the Jordan in the Spring, when it had apparently overflown its banks, they put to flight all who opposed them to the east and west, and found their way to David. We, too, need to endure hardness as good soldiers of Christ, overcome all hindrances, defeat all foes, and be ready to serve our Lord.

The Blessing of Moses.

Moses, in blessing the tribes, is in full agreement with Jacob concerning Gad, and very accurate in his predictions. He rightly attributes to God the prosperity of the tribe. It was not by their own prowess that they were able to obtain such large territories.

It is good for us always to acknowledge that any measure of success we have in life is to be traced to the bountiful hand of God.

Regarding the Gadites, as concerning all Israel, the Psalmist correctly writes:

"They got not the land in possession by their own sword,
Neither did their own arm save them,
But Thy right hand, and Thine arm,
And the light of Thy countenance,
Because Thou wast favourable unto them"

(Psa. **44**. **3**).

Scripture Parallels

Referring, no doubt, to Gad's extensive possessions in Gilead which were further enlarged by their conquest of the Hagarites, Moses says:

"Blessed is He that enlargeth Gad."

The Hebrew word *marchibh*, translated "enlarges," means literally "makes wide." It is "makes wide or spacious Gad's territory. Gives them large possessions," as was the case in Gilead.

As a substantive this word is used by David (Psa. 18. 19). He says:

"He (GOD) brought me forth into a large place;
He delivered me because He delighted in me."

The Psalmist pictures his deliverance as being put into a spacious place, where he has freedom of movement.

The same portraiture is used in Psa. 118. 5, concerning Israel's deliverance from the confederacy of nations in the last world war, spoken of as "the time of Jacob's trouble."

"Out of my distress I called upon Jah,
Jah answered me in a wide place."

The idea is that, out of a cramped, narrow gorge where they are besieged, they are liberated and brought into a wide plain where they have liberty of action.

As with the tribe of Gad so with the people of Israel. By God's gracious interposition both are delivered, and given spacious possessions, where they shall enjoy liberty to serve Him.

Foreseeing their warlike characteristics Moses adds,

"He dwelleth as a lion,
And teareth the arm with the crown of the head."

Then with reference to their request that the portion of Gilead should be given them, and was allotted to them by Moses, he continues,

"He provides the first part for himself,
There was the Law-giver's portion reserved,
He came with the heads of the people,
He executed the justice of the Lord,
And his judgment with Israel."

that is, in helping them to conquer the Canaanite nations.

After many struggles and defeats the tribe of Gad were taken into captivity by the Assyrians and placed in Halah, Habor, Hara, and by the river Gozan. Scripture assures them, however, a hopeful future. Gad's name is among the tribes sealed in Rev. 7, and Ezekiel assigns them a place in the restored land of Israel on the extreme south (Ezek. 48. 27, 28). Thus, after being overcome they will overcome at the last. This is true, of course, not only of Gad, but also of the whole Israel nation in whom God's restoring grace will be wonderfully exhibited.

The Rabbis explain (v. 21), "There was the Law-giver's portion reserved," as referring to the burial place of Moses, which they say was in Gad's territory. The word we translate "reserved," literally means "covered"—hence hidden; this they take to refer to the fact that Moses' grave remained unknown to any one. According to Joshua 13. 20, however, Pisgah was allotted to Reuben.

"He came with the heads of the people,"

may refer to the Gadites coming to Moses in order to request the land of Gilead, or to crossing the Jordan armed to help the other tribes in their wars with the Canaanites, and thus execute the righteous decrees of God and His judgments with Israel.

Moses thus commends them for promising to help their brethren settle into the land before they went back to their own inheritance on the other side of Jordan.

There is always a promise of blessing for the obedient, and a threatening of penalty for the disobedient,

> "If ye be willing and obedient, ye shall eat the good of the land, but if ye refuse and rebel ye shall be devoured with the sword" (Isa. 1. 19, 20).

was God's exhortation to Israel.

For the followers of Christ the same principle holds good:

> "Therefore, whosoever heareth these sayings of Mine and doeth them, I will liken him unto a wise man, which built his house upon a rock; And the rain descended, and the floods came, and the winds blew, and beat upon that house; and it fell not; for it was founded upon a rock. And every one that heareth these saying of Mine, and doeth them not, shall be likened unto a foolish man, which built his house upon the sand; And the rain descended, and the floods came, and the winds blew, and beat upon that house; and it fell: and great was the fall of it" (Matt. 7. 24-27).

BLESS'D tribe of Gad, when Israel sick,
    Sought by physician's skill,
And found the balm which healed their wounds
    On fragrant Gilead-hill.

Troops of disease assailed thee then ;
    To scale thy heights they passed ;
But Gilead's balm gave health to all.
    " Gad overcame at last."

Now all in vain we seek for cure,
    O Gilead, on thy brow ;
For Him Whose grace was Gilead's balm
    Thy nation hateth now.

Not even the types of health and joy
    Within thy land remain ;
The thorn and thistle have o'erspread
    The mountain and the plain.

Messiah, He is Gilead's balm,
    He poured for man His blood.
O tribes of Israel, welcome Him,
    Welcome the Christ of God.

Long have thy foes, troop upon troop,
    Their chains around thee cast ;
But welcome Him, and thou art free !
    " Gad overcame at last."

ANON.

CHAPTER XI

Asher—Happiness

" Of Asher, his bread shall be fat,
   And he shall yield royal dainties "
                              (Gen. 49. 20).

" Let Asher be blessed among the sons ;
   Let him be acceptable to his brethren,
   And let him dip his foot in oil,
   Iron and brass (copper) shall be thy bars,
   And as thy days shall be thy rest "
                              (Deut. 33. 24, 25).

CHAPTER XI

Asher—Happiness

NO play is here put upon the name of Asher, but the blessing bestowed upon the tribe fully bears out its meaning.

At the time of Asher's birth Leah sought to embody in his name her feelings of gratification, and said: "Happy am I, for the daughters will think me happy, and she called his name Asher" (Happy) (Gen. 30. 13). Asher's portion consisted more of earthly felicity than of spiritual blessedness, the latter cannot, however, be excluded.

The portion of territory allotted to that tribe comprised the lowlands, from Carmel, along the Mediterranean coast up to Zidon, and was a most fertile piece of land, rich in corn, oil and wine.

As is frequently the case, their prosperity made them self-satisfied and ease loving; they became friendly with their heathen neighbours, and were influenced by their idolatrous practices. They did not drive out the Canaanites, but dwelt among them (Judges 1. 31, 32). While some of the other tribes were fighting against Sisera, Asher took no part in the war, they remained on the seashore, and abode in their ports or river recesses, as Deborah complained (Judges 5. 17).

Once only is it recorded that they took part in war, when they joined Naphtali and Manasseh in pursuit of the Midianites, in their battle with Gideon (Judges

7. 23). They also supplied forty thousand warriors to acclaim David king (1 Chron. 12. 36).

The Prediction of Moses.

The blessing Moses pronounced on Asher was very similar to that of Jacob:

"Let Asher be blessed among the sons;
Let him be acceptable to his brethren,
And let him dip his foot in oil,
Iron and brass be thy bars,
And as thy days be thy rest" (Deut. 33. 24, 25).

Moses does not use here the word *Esher*—happiness—which is of the same root as the tribe's name, but the word *Baruch*, which is a higher form of blessing. This latter expression is employed in Scripture as blessedness of God and man, but Asher is always applied to *man's* happiness, never to God, the only possible exception is Psa. 72. 17, where it is referred to the Messiah, but this, too, has Solomon as a background.

The blessings Moses bestows upon Asher are mostly temporal, they nevertheless hold also spiritual promises, the enjoyment of favour with God and man. Many of God's children have legitimately drawn comfort and encouragement from this passage of Scripture.

Later in the chapter, Moses uses the word for happiness that is derived from the same root as the name Asher, and applies it to the whole nation.

"Happy art thou, O Israel,
Who is like unto thee, O people saved by Jehovah,
Who is the shield of thy help,
And the sword of thy excellency" (Deut. 33. 29).

Is not this true of all who worship Jehovah through His Beloved Son?

How Happiness is to be Obtained

THE LESSON OF ASHER—ILLUSTRATIONS OF
HAPPINESS.

It is very instructive that the same word, *esher*,
"felicity," is afterwards used of those who are saved
by Jehovah. It is sometimes employed in other
parts of the Bible, but it is mostly found in the book
of Psalms, which commences with this very word.
(*a*) True happiness is bestowed upon those who shun
the companionship of the wicked.

"Blessed is (or, O the happiness, *ashere* of) the man
That walketh not in the counsel of the ungodly,
Nor standeth in the way of sinners,
Nor sitteth in the seat of the scornful,
But whose delight is in the law of Jehovah."

(*b*) It teaches that true happiness comes from a
knowledge of sins forgiven, as in Psa. 32. 1, 2:

"O, the happiness (*ashere*) of him whose transgression is forgiven, whose sin is covered,
Happy (*ashere*) is the man unto whom the Lord
imputeth not iniquity,
And in whose spirit is no guile."

(*c*) It sets forth the happiness that comes from covenant relationship with God (Psa. 33. 12).

"Happy (*ashere*) is that nation, whose God is
Jehovah,
And the people whom He hath chosen for His own
inheritance."

(*d*) It further teaches the blessedness of communion
with God (Psa. 65. 4).

"Happy (*ashere*) is he whom Thou choosest,
And causest to approach unto Thee,
That He may dwell in Thy courts,
That we may be satisfied with the goodness of
Thy house,
The sanctity of Thy temple."

(e) It speaks of the felicity of having God as the source of our strength (Psa. 84. 5):

"O, the happiness (ashere) of the man whose strength is in Thee,
In whose heart are highways for Thee."

(f) It expresses the joy that comes from true piety (Psa. 112. 1):

"Happy (ashere) is the man who feareth (reverences) Jehovah,
Who greatly delights in His commandments."

(g) It also refers to the happiness of service (Isa. 32. 20):

"Happy (ashere) are ye that sow beside all waters,
That send forth the feet of the ox and the ass"

(that is, laden with grain, as these animals were the carriers of produce).

New Testament Parallels.

It is further most interesting to notice that the Greek version of the LXX, translates in all the above cases this Hebrew word *esher*, by *makarios*, that was so frequently on the lips of our Lord. This word, like its Hebrew equivalent *esher*, is generally used of men; the only exception appears to be in 1 Tim. 1. 11, and 6. 15. The Greek *eulogetos* is the equivalent of the Hebrew *baruch*, "to bless."

Thus He commenced His teaching an the Mount of Beatitudes, using the plural. (The Hebrew term is always in the plural). He repeated it many times.

"Blessed (*makarioi*) are the poor in spirit.
Blessed (*makarioi*) are they that mourn.
Blessed (*makarioi*) are the meek," etc., etc.

And when our Lord speaks again in resurrection glory, and completes the volume of Revelation, He has this word, which so characterised His ministry, again on His lips:

"Behold I come quickly, Blessed (*makarios*) is he
that keepeth the words of this prophecy of this
book" (Rev. 22. 7),

taking us back to chapter 1. 3, and finally,

"Blessed (*makarioi*) are they that wash their robes
that they may have the authority to come to the
tree of life, and may enter in by the gates into
the city."

Asher's Responsiveness.

The inspired chronicler left it on record (2 Chron.
30) that after the northern kingdom of the ten tribes
was taken into captivity by the Assyrians, Hezekiah
sent out messengers with letters to all parts of the
land of Israel, inviting those who were left to come to
Jerusalem and take part in a special celebration of
the Passover Feast he was preparing.

While many of Israel scorned, and mocked at the
messengers, some from Asher, Zebulun, and Manasseh,
humbled themselves and came to Jerusalem to keep
the feast as commanded in the Law. This, further,
resulted in a reformation among the remnant of Israel,
for after the feast these men from the ten tribes
returned to their cities, and broke in pieces the images,
cut down the groves, threw down the high places and
altars of the false deities, and utterly destroyed them
all.

Some of these Asherites evidently survived right
to the time of our Lord, for we learn from Luke's
Gospel that the aged widow and prophetess, Anna,
the daughter of Phanuel, was known to be of the tribe
of Asher (Luke 2. 36).

A Picture of Happiness.

We are not informed of what tribe Simeon was,
but we are told that he was righteous and devout,
looking for the consolation of Israel, and that the Holy

Spirit was upon him; and, further, it was revealed
to him by the Holy Spirit that he should not see death
till he had seen the Lord's Christ. This man, evidently a prophet, had the happiness of taking the
Child Jesus in his arms, blessing God, and saying:

> "Sovereign Lord (*despota*), Now lettest Thou Thy
> bondslave (*doulon*) depart in peace, according to
> Thy word, for mine eyes have seen Thy salvation
> (*soterion*) . . .
> A light to lighten the Gentiles and the glory of
> Thy people Israel" (Luke 2. 25-32).

In this happiness the daughter of Asher (happy) was
able to join, for she also gave thanks to God for this
Child, and spake of Him to all them that were looking
for the redemption of Jerusalem.

If Simeon, like Mary, was of the tribe of Judah,
which formed the great majority of the people as
no other tribe is mentioned in connection with him,
Anna, of Asher, was a representative of Israel, the ten
tribes, while Zacharias represented the Levitical
tribe. He also was filled with the Holy Ghost, and
prophesied concerning the redemption of his people.
We thus get a lovely picture of representatives from
all sections of Israel, rejoicing in the birth of their
Messiah.

The happiness of Asher will be complete when the
whole nation is restored to Christ, for his name
appears among the sealed tribes in Rev. 7. He has
a portion of land allotted to him in the restored
Palestine (Ezek. 48. 2), and the tribe is also inscribed on the gates of the new city whose name will
be *Jehovah Shammah*, "The Lord is there."

The prayer of Moses for Asher was that he might
live in peace with the other tribes and enjoy their
good will. This is indeed a blessing that brings
happiness.

To such an extent did the ancients appreciate the benefits of peace that they embodied it in their ordinary salutations when they met one another. *Shalom aleychem*, "peace be unto you," was the greeting, and the response was, *aleychem shalom*, "upon you be peace." In Scripture it is spoken of as asking each other of peace. [Exod. 18. 7 (*margin*), and Judges 18. 15, where it is translated "and saluted him," the Hebrew is, "And they asked him of peace."]

This wish is implied in the words of Moses,
"Let Asher be blessed among the sons,
    Let him be acceptable to his brethren."

These words truly describe Asher's characteristic, he was peaceably inclined and not at all quarrelsome, like some of the other tribes.

The world still longs for the blessing of peace, but it does not, and will not enjoy it till our Lord, the Prince of Peace, returns and sets up His reign of peace and equity. Thank God, however, that as individual followers of Christ, it is possible for us to enjoy it already. Did not the Lord Jesus say:
"Peace I leave with you; My peace I give unto you; not as the world giveth give I unto you. Let not your heart be troubled, neither let it be afraid" (John 14. 27).

The world gave its peace in a salutation that was a mere form of speech without any depth of meaning, as we, nowadays, say to those we meet, "How do you do?" When Christ gives His peace He gives it actually and truly. With His words He really imparts the blessing indicated by them for us to enjoy.

Further, in agreement with Jacob's blessing:
"Asher, his bread shall be fat,
    And he shall yield royal dainties,"
Moses says,

"Let him dip his foot in oil. "

Both of them refer to the great fertility of Asher's portion of the land.   The connection between these two passages of Scripture is still clearer in the original, where the word for "fat" comes from the same root as the word "oil. "   The one is *Shemenah*, the other is *Shemen*.

For our temporal prosperity, yea, for our daily bread, as for our spiritual mercies, we are dependent upon God.   His invisible fingers work and manipulate under the ground, changing the single grain into the number that there may be seed for the sower and bread for the eater, and we have reason to pray, "Give us this day our daily bread. "

Lastly Moses says :

"Iron and brass (copper) be thy shoes,
And as thy days be thy rest. "

Some translate it "Iron and copper, shall be thy bars, " the fact is, that both words *shoes* and *bars* come from the same root *naal*, but the word "bar" seems to suit the context better.   The blessing of Moses is threefold : peace, prosperity, and protection, and these would bring him rest.

As long as the tribes were in communion with God all these blessings were theirs, and when they forsook their God they were deprived of them, but when they become reconciled with their Messiah and Saviour, their present sufferings will come to an end, and again they will enjoy these blessings in rich measure.   The promise of Joel 2. 19 will be verified to them.

"Behold, I will send you corn and wine and oil,
And ye shall be satisfied therewith,
And I will no more make you a reproach among the nations. "

Again:
"And it shall come to pass in that day,
That the mountains shall drop down sweet wine,
And the hills shall flow with milk,
And all the brooks of Judah shall flow with water,
And a fountain shall come forth from the house
of Jehovah.
And shall water the valley of Shittim . . .
And Judah shall abide for ever,
And Jerusalem from generation to generation,
And I will cleanse their bloodguiltiness that I
have not cleansed,
For Jehovah dwelleth in Zion" (Joel 3. 18-21).

A LAND of plenty Asher had,
With olive-grove and vineyard clad ;
And God's own promise as his plea
That " as his days his strength should be."

Enamoured of the fertile soil,
He dipped his foot in corn and oil ;
To ease he gave his soul a prey,
In sloth he spent probation's day.

Supine amid his folds he lay,
And slept the promised strength away ;
Nor ventured on the mighty plea,
" And as thy days thy strength shall be."

For this Assyria's eagle came,
For this, in land of unknown name,
His coward sloth and guilty fears
He mourns with unavailing tears.

But not for aye.   From sands and snow
Of Orient pilgrim streams shall flow ;
And Jacob's sons shall turn again
To the returning latter rain.

.   .   .   .   .

Awake, ye slumberers in Zion ;
Think not that *ease* is happiness !
But seek the rest of Judah's Lion
When He shall come, the Prince of Peace "

PAULIN.

CHAPTER XII

Naphtali—The Wrestler

" Naphtali is a hind let loose,
  That giveth forth goodly sayings " (Gen. 49. 21).

" And of Naphtali he said,
  O Naphtali, satisfied with favour,
  And full of the blessing of Jehovah,
  Possess thou the sea and the south (or sunny region)."
                                    (Deut. 33. 23.)

CHAPTER XII

Naphtali—The Wrestler

A S in the case of the other sons of Jacob, the meaning of Naphtali's name was indicated at his nativity. When Bilhah gave birth to this, her second son, Rachel, in a tone of triumph, exclaimed, "With mighty wrestlings (*naphiule*) have I wrestled (*niphtalti*) with my sister, and have prevailed, and she called his name Naphtali (my wrestling) (Gen. 30. 8).

Naphtule Elohim means literally "with the wrestlings of God." The Authorised Version nevertheless expresses the idiom of the original.

Elohim and El are names for God, but as God is the all-powerful and the all-reverent, these names are sometimes used in the sense of strength or greatness, as in Psa. 36. 6, *Harerey El*, "mountains of God," *i.e.*, lofty mountains, and Psa. 80. 10, *Arzey El*, "cedars of God," *i.e.*, mighty cedars. This is in accordance with the root meaning of these words.

Wrestling in Prayer.

There evidently was some rivalry between the two sisters in seeking to get and retain Jacob's affection. The Jewish Rabbis and Chaldaic Paraphrases may, however, be quite correct in saying that Rachel refers to her wrestling in prayer. This is what we need to do in order to prevail. We should not be so often defeated by the enemy if we were more given to earnest, importunate prayer. The men and women who obtained the greatest spiritual victories, were men and women who knew how to wrestle with God in prayer.

For our instruction and encouragement the inspired evangelist records that the Lord Jesus, when He met with the opposition of the Pharisees, "went out into the mountain to pray; and continued all night in prayer to God" (Luke 6. 12). By so doing, our Lord set us an example in harmony with His teaching that "men ought always to pray and not to faint."

The Wrestling of Jacob.

Naphtali's father was also a wrestler in this higher sense. As it is related in Gen. 32, a mysterious being appeared to Jacob and wrestled with him, He is called *Ish*, "a man," and the prophet Hosea, who gives us a divinely inspired comment on this incident (12. 2-5), speaks of him as an "Angel", also as "Jehovah, God of Hosts." Jacob also speaks of Him as "*Elohim*," God.

Hosea, moreover, tells us that Jacob's wrestling with Him was "weeping and supplication," and further, that by his strength, that is, by his persistence and importunity, crying, "I will not let Thee go except Thou bless me," Jacob prevailed. He was in desperate need, and his earnest prayer brought him the blessing and victory, for he saw God face to face, and his soul was preserved. And truly Jacob's greatest triumph was when the Angel touched the hollow of his thigh, setting it out of joint and disabling him from going his own way.

The Apostle Paul earnestly besought the brethren in Rome that they should strive (agonise) with himself in prayer for him (Rom. 15. 30).

Epaphras is likewise said to have striven, contended (Greek, agonised) in prayer for the Colossians (Col. 4. 12). All these were great wrestlers.

Some need to wrestle for salvation; if they do as Jacob, they too are sure to prevail, for He Who has made known to them their desperate need, is near at hand to deliver. Indeed He invites such to take hold of His strength and make peace with Him (Isa. 27. 5).

Others need to wrestle for grace that they may overcome some besetment which they cannot resist in their own strength; for such God "will with the temptation also make a way of escape."

Still others need to wrestle for blessing in service, for them there is the gracious promise, "Lo, I am with you alway; even unto the end of the age" (Matt. 28. 20). But in all our wrestling we need to remember that the race is not to the swift, nor the battle to the strong, but God's strength is made perfect in weakness.

We are told little about the disposition of Naphtali himself, but the name seems to indicate the character of the tribe.

In the wilderness journey, Naphtali and Asher marched together under the standard of Dan, who was Naphtali's full brother. During the forty years in the wilderness the tribe decreased in number by 8,000 men; from 53,400 to 45,400. Whether that was in wrestling with the enemies from other nations that opposed Israel, or by falling victims to the enemies in their own evil hearts, and dying in consequence by the pestilence (Num. 11. 33), we cannot say.

Naphtali's Valour.

In the war against Sisera the people of Naphtali played an important part, and were praised for it by Deborah (Judges 5. 18). Barak, the leader in that battle, was of Kadesh Naphtali.

This tribe also readily responded to Gideon in his struggle against the Midianites (Judges 6. 35; 7. 23).

Out of Naphtali came a thousand captains and 37,000 men, armed with shield and spear, to make David king over all Israel. They also joined the other northern tribes in providing cattle, and flour, and fruit, and wine, and oil, for the coronation festivities (1 Chron. 12. 34, 40).

Naphtali's Loosened Feet.

Jacob likens Naphtali to a hind let loose, giving forth goodly sayings. The picture is that of a gazelle set free from some entanglement in the jungle to run about freely as it loves to do.

When Christ sets us free we become free indeed from the entanglements of the world, ready to run swiftly on His errands.

The Bible often compares people to the hind, *Asahel*, in his swiftness is likened to the sure footed roe, or hind (2 Sam. 2. 18). The warlike Gadites, who came to support David in Ziklag, are said to have been "as the roes upon the mountains" (1 Chron. 12. 8). The prophet Habakkuk completes his prophecies by declaring his great joy in the Lord, because He will be his strength and make his feet swift like those of the hinds to walk with good tidings of salvation upon the high places (Hab. 3. 18, 19).

In the Song of Solomon (2. 8) we get a beautiful picture of the beloved Bridegroom coming joyfully and swiftly to His people like the roe or a young hart, leaping over the mountains and skipping over the hills. The Jews in their prayers make this a picture of Messiah's coming to Israel. But the Coming of Christ is also the hope of His Church, yea, and the blessing of the world.

The Septuagint translates Gen. 49. 21:
"Naphtali is a spreading tree (stem)
Bestowing beauty on its fruit. "

This does not show that the translators of the Greek Bible had a different text before them, but that they had the same text without the present vowel points, and by supplying other vowels gave the words a different meaning. Thus, instead of *ayyalah*, "a hind, " they read *aylah*, "a big tree. " *Shelucha*—literally, "sent forth, " they translate figuratively "spread forth"; *imerey*, "sayings, " they read *amirey*, "boughs. "

The Samaritan Pentateuch, which is considered very reliable, agrees with the Hebrew text.

Jonathan's Chaldee paraphrase also supports the Hebrew. It adds: "Naphtali is a swift messenger like a hind that runneth on the top of the mountains bringing good tidings" (Cant. 2. 8, 9).

The Jerusalem paraphrase is quite similar and confirms our version. These Targumim apply the sentence: "He giveth goodly words, " to Naphtali, who, they declare, brought to Jacob the good tidings that Joseph was still alive.

Christ's Teachings, Goodly Sayings.

The Spirit of God gave the Patriarch a vision of what was to take place in the land of Naphtali in the days of Christ, Who carried on His marvellous ministry and sublime teaching in that district. It is generally considered that the Mount of Beatitudes, where Christ spoke those grand and heart searching words to His disciples, was near Safed, in Naphtali. These were truly goodly sayings.

Isaiah 9. 1 speaks of Galilee, where the great spiritual light was to appear, as the land of Zebulun and Naphtali. It was on a mountain in Galilee, therefore, probably in Naphtali, that Christ assembled His disciples after His resurrection, and gave them the commission to go with the goodly words into all the world.

Those who so astonished the crowds on the day of Pentecost when they spoke to them under the influence of the Holy Spirit in the various languages of their own lands, were Galileans, most likely, of Naphtali. These also carried the goodly words of the Gospel into the different countries where they were scattered by the persecution. Truly, to them were applicable the words of the prophet:

"How beautiful upon the mountains are the feet of him that bringeth good tidings, that publisheth peace; that bringeth good tidings of good, that publisheth salvation; that saith unto Zion, Thy God reigneth!" (Isa. 52. 7).

The Meaning of Moses' Blessing.

Much of Naphtali's history was a struggle, nevertheless it was not without advantages. This is indicated by Moses.

"O Naphtali, satisfied with favour,
And full of blessing of the Lord,
Possess thou the sea and the south (or sunny region)" (Deut. 33. 23).

Commentators have found some difficulty in this verse, because Naphtali's inheritance lay on the north and not on the west of the promised land. But the Hebrew *yam*, which is here translated "west," primarily means the sea; only because the west was bounded by the sea it was called *yam* "sea," and sometimes *yammah*, "seaward." There are other Hebrew words for west, as *maarabh* and *mebho hashshemesh*. Here *yam* should be translated "sea" in its primary meaning, and not "west." This is then true to fact, for a great part of Naphtali's land was bounded by the Sea of Galilee.

Also the word *Darom* here translated "south," means the "sunny region," hence the south quarter where the sun shines most. (See Gesenius' Heb. Lexicon). This was also quite true of Naphtali. The southern section of that tribe is called the garden of Palestine, the little plains along the shore of the Sea of Galilee are of unrivalled fertility. Josephus speaks of Gennesaret, on the shore of that sea, as an earthly paradise where the choicest fruits grow luxuriously, and where eternal Spring reigns.

The northern portion of Naphtali is mountainous, reaching a height of nearly 4,000 feet; it includes Safed, which is supposed to be the "city set on a hill that cannot be hid"; also Kadesh, one of the cities of refuge which was apportioned to the Gershonites. It also formed the headquarters of Barak at the time of the war with Sisera.

Naphtali's lowlands include Lake Merom and the fertile district of Huleh, which the Jews have recently purchased for cultivation.

Naphtali Satisfied with Favour and Full of Jehovah's Blessing.

While this takes us back to the promise given to this tribe by Jacob, and was verified to them in the fertile portion of land allotted to them, it is yet to be fulfilled to them in a higher sense when the Lord shall redeem Jacob and ransom him from the hand of him that is stronger than he. When

"They shall come and sing in the height of Zion, and shall flow together to the goodness of Jehovah, for wheat, and for wine, and for oil, and for the young of the flock, and of the herd, and their souls shall be as a watered garden, and they shall not sorrow any more at all . . .

And I will satiate the soul of the priests with fatness, and My people shall be satisfied with My goodness, saith Jehovah" (Jer. 31. 11-14).

Ratson, the word translated "favour," means good will or acceptance, as in Isa. 61. 2, "The acceptable year of Jehovah." It takes us on to a time when Naphtali and the whole nation will find acceptance with God through Christ and will enjoy in fulness the blessing of Jehovah. With Christ upon the throne they shall also possess the sea and the south, *i.e.*, sea and land. The south which is now desert, shall, under the blessed reign of Messiah, be made to "rejoice and blossom as the rose."

How beauteous are their feet
  Who stand on Zion's hill !
Who bring salvation on their tongues,
  And words of peace reveal !

How charming is their voice !
  How sweet their tidings are !
" Zion, behold thy Saviour King ;
  He reigns and triumphs here."

How happy are our ears,
  That hear this joyful sound,
Which kings and prophets waited for,
  And sought, but never found.

How blessed are our eyes,
  That see this Heavenly light !
Prophets and kings desired it long,
  But died without the sight.

The watchman join their voice,
  And tuneful notes employ ;
Jerusalem breaks forth in songs,
  And deserts learn the joy.

The Lord makes bare His arm
  Through all the earth abroad ;
Let every nation now behold
  Their Saviour and their God.

ISAAC WATTS.

CHAPTER XIII

Joseph—Addition

" Joseph is a fruitful bough,
A fruitful bough by a fountain,
Branches running over the wall.
And the archers embittered his life,
They shot at him and hated him.
But his bow abode in strength,
And the arms of his hands were made agile,
From the hands of the Mighty One of Jacob.
From thence is the Shepherd, the Stone of Israel ;
Even from the God of thy fathers, Who will help
     thee,
And from the Almighty, Who will bless thee ;
With blessings of Heaven above,
Blessings of the deep lying beneath,
Blessings of the breasts and of the womb.
The blessings of thy father have surpassed the
     blessings of my progenitors.
Unto the utmost bound of the everlasting hills
They shall be upon the head of Joseph,
And upon the crown of the head of him that was
     separate from his brethren."

(Gen. 49. 22-26).

CHAPTER XIII

Joseph—Addition
Christ and Joseph.

WHAT a wonderful story is Joseph's, how strikingly it foreshadows the experience of our Lord! The Bible is full of types and adumbrations as well as direct predictions of Christ. Men, places, and even material objects are all used to point, as with a finger, to the Coming Christ.

"The Cross of our Lord Jesus Christ," says an esteemed expositor, "is the centre of human history. It is the sun around which the firmament circles; the key to all Scripture, history and type; the fact which gives meaning to all other facts. To ignore the Cross is to repeat the error of the old philosophers; who thought that the earth, and not the sun, was the centre of our system, and to whom, therefore, the very heavens were in confusion. To know and love the Cross—to stand beside it as the faithful women did when Jesus died—is to obtain a deep insight into the harmonies of all things in Heaven and earth . . .

"The Great Artist of all things, enamoured with the wondrous Cross, filled the world with foreshadowings and anticipations of it long before it stood with outstretched arms on the little hill of Calvary . . .

"The sun which now shines, so to speak, from the other side of the Cross, so as to fling its shadow forward clear and sharp on the canvas of the present, once shone from where we now stand, and flung its

shadow backward upon the canvas of the past.   One
of these shadows is caught and photographed for us
in this sweet story of Joseph."—*F. B. Meyer.*

The life of Joseph specially abounded to such an
extent in incidents that were similar to those that
took place in the life of Christ, that the Bible student
is forced to the conclusion that it was written on
purpose to prefigure Him of Whom all the Scriptures
bear witness.

Striking Parallels.

Without entering into details we mention a few of
the parallel incidents.

Joseph loved by his father (Gen. 37. 3).
God Himself declared His great love for His Son
(Matt. 3. 17).
Joseph disapproved of his brethren's evil dis-
courses (Gen. 37. 2).
So the Lord Jesus did of the Pharisees (Luke 12. 1).
Joseph hated by his brethren for it (Gen. 37. 4).
This was also true of Jesus (John 7. 7).
His brothers envied him (Gen. 37. 11).
It was for envy they delivered Christ (Matt. 27. 18)
Joseph's greatness was predicted (Gen. 37. 7-10).
The Bible is full of predictions of Christ's great-
ness, but see specially Luke 1. 32.
Joseph sent to seek the welfare of his brothers
(Gen. 37. 14).
So was our Lord (John 5. 30, 36).
Joseph obeyed and went to them, though at
some risk (Gen. 37. 12).
So did Christ (Matt. 21. 37, 39; John 16. 28).
Joseph was separated from his brethren (Gen.
49. 26; Deut. 33. 16).
Christ was also "holy, guileless, undefiled, and
separated from sinners, and made higher than
the Heavens "(Heb. 7. 26).

Joseph's brethren planned to put him to death (Gen. 37. 20).

This was done by the scribes and Pharisees to our Lord (Matt. 21. 38; 26. 3, 4).

Joseph was sold as a slave (Gen. 37. 28).

Jesus was sold for the price of a slave (Matt. 26. 15).

Joseph was tempted but did not yield (Gen. 39. 8, 9).

So Christ (Matt. 4. 10). The prince of this world had nothing in Him (John 14. 30; Heb. 4. 15).

Joseph was falsely accused (Gen. 39. 17, 18).

So was Christ (Mark 14. 56, 57).

Joseph was wrongfully condemned (Gen. 39. 20).

Jesus also (Matt. 26. 66).

Concerning Joseph the brethren said, "Come, let us kill him " (Gen. 37. 20).

Christ quoted these words of Himself, "Let us kill Him" (Matt. 21. 38).

Joseph was thought dead but was alive (Gen. 37. 33).

Christ has been thought dead but is alive (Rev. 1. 18).

Joseph was called the revealer of secrets (Gen. 41. 15, 16).

Our Lord was that in the highest degree (Luke 10. 22).

Joseph was exalted after his humiliation (Gen. 41. 40-44).

Christ was exalted a Prince and a Saviour (Acts 5. 31).

Joseph opened the stores and fed the people (Gen. 41. 56).

Christ fed the hungry (Matt. 14. 19-21; John 6. 11).

Joseph's brethren confessed their guilt (Gen. 42. 21).

The Jews will also confess their guilt and repent (Zech. 12. 10).

Joseph's brethren were reconciled to him (Gen. 45. 15).

So will Israel be reconciled to Christ (Rom. 11. 26).

Joseph was made ruler and saviour of Egypt, a Gentile people.

The Lord Jesus opened the door of the Kingdom to the Gentiles and became their Saviour and Lord.

The diligent student of Scripture will find many more parallels in the story of Joseph and of our Lord.

The name of Joseph is significant. When, at his birth, Rachel gave him that name she put double play upon it; first she said, "God hath taken away my reproach," then, "Jehovah shall add to me another son" (Gen. 30. 23, 24).

The Hebrew word for "taken away," is *asaph*, and the word for "shall add" is *Yoseph*, very similar in sound. Yoseph expresses a wish, and was prophetic, for God did give her another son—Benjamin, but Joseph's whole life was predictive of the other Benjamin, the Son of God's right hand, as that name means, the other Child to be born and Son to be given, Who is also the Mighty God and Everlasting Father (Isa. 9. 6); He shall indeed take away the reproach of His people (Isa. 25. 8). The word "rebuke" in this verse is the same as is translated "reproach" in Gen. 30. 23, and is thus correctly rendered in the Revised Version.

Joseph's Title.

Pharaoh surnamed Joseph, Zaphnath Paaneah, which some translate "Revealer of secrets"; others, more in harmony with the Greek Septuagint *Psonthomphanech*, think it denotes "Saviour of the World." In either of these meanings the words are applicable,

in the first place to Joseph, and in a deeper sense to
our Lord, Who is the Great Revealer. "In Him are
hid all the treasures of wisdom and knowledge"
(Col. 2. 3). He Himself declared:

> "No one knoweth Who the Son is save the Father,
> and Who the Father is save the Son, and he to
> whomsoever the Son willeth to reveal Him"
> (Luke 10. 22. See also John 17. 6-8, 25, 26).

Joseph might have been called the saviour of the
world, because he was the means of preserving the
people from starvation, but concerning the Lord Jesus
we can repeat with great assurance the words of the
Samaritans,

> "We know that this is indeed the Christ, the
> Saviour of the world" (John 4. 42).

From Prisoner to Prince.

What a wonderful change that was in Joseph's
position! From a slave in an Egyptian prison, to
rule over the whole country. He is described as being
arrayed in fine linen, with a gold chain about his neck,
and Pharaoh's ring on his finger, seated in the royal
chariot, and a herald running before him proclaiming
Abrech, "Bow the knee"—do him homage! (Gen.
41. 41-3).

How we rejoice that our Lord Who made Himself
of no reputation, took upon Himself the form of a
servant, and became obedient unto death, even the
death of the Cross, is now also highly exalted, for
God has given Him,

> "A name which is above every name; That at (or in)
> the Name of Jesus every knee should bow, of things
> in Heaven, and things on earth, and things under
> the earth, and that every tongue should confess
> that Jesus Christ is Lord to the glory of God the
> Father" (Phil. 2. 7-11).

Our Lord is raised from the lowest point of humiliation to the highest pinnacle of exaltation and His sway will be over all peoples, nations, and languages.

Picturesque Hebrew.

Jacob, in blessing Joseph, describes him poetically as a fruitful bough by a fountain whose branches run over the wall, a beautiful picture of fertility.

The original, here, for "bough," is *ben*, "son," and for branches," *banoth*, "daughters." In the picturesque Hebrew the expressions, "branch," and "son," are sometimes interchanged; for as the branch is the outgrowth of the tree and partakes of its life, nature, and strength, so the son is the offspring of the father and partakes of his life, nature, and strength. The son of a tree is, of course, a branch, and the branch of a human being is a son.

Thus the Messiah, in His humanity is figuratively called the Branch or Sprout of David (Jer. 23. 5), and in His Deity the Branch of Jehovah (Isa. 4. 2), for He is both the Son of David and the Son of God.

A further illustration of this is found in Psa. 80, where Israel is likened to a vine brought out of Egypt and planted in the promised land, but it having become waste, the Psalmist prays,

"Look down from Heaven and behold and visit this vine; and the vineyard which Thy right hand hath planted, and the branch that Thou madest strong for Thyself" (vv. 13, 14). The word "branch" in the Heb. is *ben*, "son," but being of a vine it is rightly translated "branch."

Our Lord is often brought before us under the figure of a branch. In His humility He is likened to a pliant suckling and root out of a dry ground (Isa. 53. 2). But this tender twig that is taken from the highest branch of the lofty cedar (*i.e.*, the Davidic

Tree), is then planted on a high and eminent mountain, in the land of Israel, and there He becomes a graceful cedar, bringing forth fruit and giving shelter to various sorts of birds (Ezek. 17. 22, 23). Similarly Isaiah brings Him before us in His royalty as a branch growing out of the root of Jesse; upon Whom rests the Spirit of Jehovah in His sevenfold fulness (Isa. 11. 1, 2).

Joseph's Numerous Descendants.

The Patriarch predicts here that Joseph's descendants would be numerous, and in this he repeats the thought that Joseph embodied in the name of Ephraim, which he gave to his second son, and which means fruitful, "God hath made me fruitful in the land of my affliction," he declared (Gen. 41. 52). Moreover, Jacob himself, in his blessing of Joseph's sons, prayed, "Let them grow into a multitude in the midst of the earth" (Gen. 48. 16). Now the prayer has become a prophecy and has been abundantly fulfilled.

Though Joseph had only two sons they wonderfully increased in Egypt and became two great tribes.

Ephraim had a fertile and important portion in the Holy Land, and Manasseh had one portion on the west of the Jordan, and leaping, stepping as it were, over the wall possessed another spacious territory in Gilead, on the east of the river.

At the Exodus, Joseph, i.e., Manasseh and Ephraim, together formed the second largest tribe of all Israel, Judah being the largest with 74,600 men of twenty years old and upward, and Manasseh and Ephraim with 72,700; and at the second census at the end of the wilderness journey, they further increased, and together they became the largest of all the tribes, with 85,200 men, while Judah, the next largest, numbered 76,500.

Joseph's Birthright.

Further, with the privilege of primogeniture given to Joseph (see 1 Chron. 5. 1, 2), he received the double portion according to Deut. 21. 17. This was indicated by Jacob when he declared that Ephraim and Manasseh would be to him as Reuben and Simeon (Gen. 48. 5). They remained, therefore, two separate tribes in the land, where Ephraim actually vied with Judah for the supremacy, while Manasseh had possessions on both sides of the Jordan. Joseph, further received an extra portion of inheritance (Gen. 48. 22). This was evidently the ancient township of Shechem (John 4. 5). There it was, therefore, that Joseph's bones were buried (Josh. 24. 32). The Hebrew word for "portion" (Gen. 48. 22) is *Shechem*, the name of this town. This accordingly formed the inheritance of Ephraim.

It must have been an important place, as it was there that Rehoboam was acclaimed King over Israel, and Jeroboam evidently enlarged it and made it the capital of his kingdom.

The most illustrious son of Ephraim was Joshua, who succeeded Moses, the Law-giver, and brought the Israelites into the Promised Land, and thus was a type of Christ Who bore the same name, and Who truly was the salvation of Jehovah, as the name denotes. He, moreover, bestows upon Jew and Gentile an eternal inheritance which the Law could never give.

CHAPTER XIV

Joseph (continued)

" And of Joseph he said,
Blessed of Jehovah be his land,
Of the precious things of Heaven, of the dew,
And of the deep that couches beneath,
And of the precious things, the produce of the sun,
And of the precious things, the growth of the months,
And of the chief things of the ancient mountains,
And of the precious things of the everlasting hills,
And of the precious things of the earth and its fulness,
And of the goodwill of Him that dwelt in the bush,
Let them come upon the head of Joseph,
And on the crown of the head of him who was
    separated from his brethren.
His glory is like the firstling of his bullock,
And his horns are like the horns of a buffalo,
With them together shall he push the peoples to the
    ends of the earth,
And they are the myriads of Ephraim,
And they are the thousands of Manasseh "

(Deut. 33. 13-17).

CHAPTER XIV

Joseph (continued)
Joseph's Prosperity.

JOSEPH'S brethren who fought against him, are compared to archers (or masters of arrows) who shot at him, but his bow abode in strength and his hands were made agile by the hands of the Mighty One of Jacob.

This is a graphic picture of Joseph's brothers' cruel contention against him, shooting their arrows to injure and destroy, and it had its parallel in the case of our Lord; as these masters of arrows shot at their brother, so did Christ's persecutors act against Him. Prophetically the Psalmist describes them as those

"Who whet their tongue like a sword,
And bend their bows to shoot their arrows,
Even bitter words.
That they may shoot in secret at the perfect.
Suddenly do they shoot at him,
And fear not" (Psa. 64. 3, 4).
"But His Bow abode in strength,
And the arms of his hands were made agile
From the hands of the Mighty One of Jacob."

Ultimately, his was the victory, as was the case with the Lord Jesus, The Psalmist continues,

"But God will shoot at them;
With an arrow suddenly shall they be wounded."

Grievous indeed was their wound, for the arrows of Christ are sharp in the hearts of the King's enemies.

Happy is the man who has the Mighty One of Jacob, not as his foe, but as his Friend, to strengthen his hands, to fight his battles, and to subdue his enemies. The Patriarch rightly attributes Joseph's successes to God. It was his father's God Who helped him, and the Almighty Who blessed him with blessings of Heaven above and the deep beneath; and blessings of a numerous posterity, beyond anything that his progenitors enjoyed, to the utmost bound of the everlasting heights. Truly, "the race is not to the swift, nor the battle to the strong," and "Happy is he that hath the God of Jacob for his help" (Eccles. 9. 11; Psa. 146. 5).

A Significant Title.

This striking title—"The Mighty One of Jacob"— *Abhir Yaakob*, takes us back to these patriarchs, and brings to our mind the wonderful way that God overruled all that happened to them, and brought them victory out of seeming defeat.

We are not surprised that this significant title is also used in other parts of Scripture.

In Isa. 1. 24 it is changed to *Abhir Israel*, "The Mighty One of Israel," and coupled with other titles, *Adon Jehovah Zebaoth*, "Lord Jehovah of Hosts." In Isa. 60. 16 it is joined with the titles Saviour and Redeemer. It predicts that the abundant blessing God will bestow on Israel will be convincing proof to them that He is their Saviour and Redeemer, "The Mighty One of Jacob." In Isa. 49. 26 the same combination of titles is found, and the promise there is that God's gracious interposition on Israel's behalf will be convincing proof to *all flesh* that He is Israel's Saviour and Redeemer, the Mighty One of Jacob. He will plead their cause and fight their battle, and thus display His redeeming love and mighty power.

Messianic Names.

One sentence here needs fuller elucidation. It is, "From thence is the Shepherd, the Stone of Israel." First, what or who is the source referred to by the expression "from thence"? Is it Jacob or Joseph, or is it God? All these are previously mentioned. A careful translation of the context will show it refers to God. We have translated it literally:

"From the hands of the Mighty One of Jacob;
From thence is the Shepherd, the Stone of Israel,
Even from the God of thy fathers, Who will help thee,
And from the Almighty Who will bless thee."

Four times is the preposition "from" used here, in the original; but in our English version it is translated "by" three times, and "from" once; the connection is, therefore, lost. It should read: "From thence is the Shepherd, the Stone of Israel, Even from the God of thy fathers, etc." The Shepherd and Stone of Israel are two Messianic titles and indicate Messiah's Divine origin. Though partially and poetically they apply to Joseph, actually and ultimately they refer to Christ.

Genesis is the book of beginnings, and many great truths are given in germ which are more fully developed in the other books of the Bible. This is true concerning the title, "The Mighty One of Jacob." It is also true regarding these designations of the Messiah. We have already noticed that Joseph, in a very remarkable degree, foreshadowed the Lord Jesus. We are therefore not surprised that Jacob, while prophesying concerning him and his posterity, should catch a glimpse of Christ, Whom he portrayed, and Who is to be the means of bringing the blessing here predicted to these tribes.

Christ as Shepherd.

Shepherd is a fitting designation of Christ. It brings to our mind the many benevolent characteristics and functions carried out by Him.

Jacob himself had been a good and skilful shepherd, under whose charge the sheep thrived and increased, for he tended them carefully, willing to endure the heat of the day and the cold of the night (Gen. 31. 40); he therefore knew the noble qualities of a shepherd and used the name as a suitable figure for the Divine Leader of men. In Gen. 48. 15 he speaks of God as feeding, or better, shepherding him (*haro-eh*) all his life long.

The prophets afterwards often describe the Messiah under this appellation. Isa. 40. 10, 11, speaks of Him as the DIVINE SHEPHERD.

> "Behold the Lord Jehovah will come forth with strength . . . He shall feed His flock like a shepherd, He shall gather the lambs with His arm and carry them in His bosom, and gently lead the suckling ewes."

This is a picture of combined strength and tenderness. Jer. 31. 10, 11 likens Him to a WATCHFUL SHEPHERD Who will re-gather and redeem His scattered flock.

Ezekiel (34. 20-5) speaks of Him as the DILIGENT SHEPHERD, in contrast to the other leaders who are negligent self-seekers.

Zechariah (13. 7) speaks of Him as the SMITTEN SHEPHERD Whom the sword of God's justice would smite, and thus open a fountain for sin and uncleanness (13. 1).

When the Lord Jesus put forth the claim that He was the GOOD SHEPHERD Who gave His life for the sheep, He gathered up all the above references, and applied them to Himself; for they were so many portraits of Him in His manifold characteristics.

This same figure is carried forward in Hebrews 13. 20, where the Lord Jesus, in His resurrection glory, is called the GREAT SHEPHERD of the sheep, and in 1 Peter 5. 4, where He is spoken of as the CHIEF SHEPHERD Who, at His Second Coming, will distribute rewards to the under shepherds who have been faithful in guiding and feeding the flock of God.

Christ the Living Stone.

The second title here mentioned—the Stone of Israel—is also one frequently applied to Christ throughout the Scriptures; it depicts stability and strength as the rock of ages. In 1 Peter 2. 4 He is called the Living Stone. Both the prophet of the Old Testament and the apostle of the New Testament, compare Him to a foundation stone upon whom rests the entire spiritual structure that He is building (Isa. 28. 16; 1 Cor. 3. 11); and indeed, other foundation can no man lay than that is laid, which is Christ. He is also the precious and ornamental Corner-Stone that will eventually crown the completed temple. At the present He is the Stone refused by His people, but one day He will take His place as the topmost Stone of the Temple, and will be welcomed by them with shoutings of "grace, grace unto it" (Psa. 118. 22; Zech. 4. 7).

Joseph Blessed by Moses.

The Blessing that Moses gives to Joseph is in complete harmony with that which Jacob gives him. This benediction is also a beautiful blending of prayer and prediction; temporal and spiritual blessings are invoked in rich abundance upon the people and the land. The benefits are drawn from many sources, from heaven above, and the deep beneath, from the ancient mountains and the everlasting heights, all are in the possession and under the control of our God. His resources are inexhaustible, and He makes them available to those who are in covenant relationship with Him, and who appropriate them by faith. These benisons are, further, to come regularly with the successive months of the year (*yerachim*), and, like the blessings given by Jacob, they include mighty and numerous descendants, which were abundantly fulfilled to Joseph.

But however great and numerous these blessings are, the privileges we have in Christ surpass them all. Well might the apostle exclaim:

"Blessed be the God and Father of our Lord Jesus Christ, Who hath blessed us with all spiritual blessings in the heavenly places in Christ" (Eph. 1. 3).

These favours had their origin in the eternal ages of the past, for in Christ, God has chosen us before the foundation of the world, and they include the highest privilege, "That we should be to the praise of His glory" (Eph. 1. 12).

The Lesson of the Burning Bush.

The central blessing to Joseph, and the greatest of them all is, that they should enjoy "the goodwill of Him that dwelt in the bush."

The mind of Moses goes back to that memorable occasion when, in the desert of Sinai, God graciously revealed Himself to him in His glory and sent him on the errand of mercy, to deliver Israel from the yoke of bondage. We are told:

"The Angel of Jehovah appeared unto him in a flame of fire out of the midst of a bush; and he looked, and behold the bush burned with fire, and the bush was not consumed" (Exod. 3. 2).

Who this Angel was we are told in verse 6:

"Moreover, He said, I am the God of thy father, the God of Abraham, the God of Isaac, and the God of Jacob. "

Jacob speaks of Him as the Angel that redeemed him; he also identifies Him with God, and invokes His blessing upon Ephraim and Manasseh (Gen. 48. 15, 16). It was God Who caused the bush to burn with fire and not consume, thus indicating to His people that they would pass through the fires of persecution in Egypt and in other lands, and not be destroyed, as He assured them later through the prophet:

"When thou passest through the waters I will be with thee; and through the rivers they shall not overflow thee; when thou walkest through the fire thou shalt not be burned; neither shall the flame kindle upon thee" (Isa. 43. 2).

Again:

"For I am with thee, saith Jehovah, to save thee; though I make a full end of all nations whither I have scattered thee, yet will I not make a full end of thee; but I will correct thee in measure, and will not leave thee altogether unpunished" (Jer. 30. 11).

Further, as God illumined the common thorn bush with the light of His Divine glory, changing by His presence the emblem of the curse into an earnest of blessing, and making it an object of splendour and of attraction, so will He cause His face to shine upon Israel when they again enjoy the goodwill of Him that dwelt in the bush (Num. 6. 25; Psa. 80. 3). He will so transform them that they, too, will reflect His glory. "Arise, shine, " cries the prophet in addressing Israel,

"For thy light is come, and the glory of Jehovah is risen upon thee. For behold, the darkness shall cover the earth, and gross darkness the peoples; but Jehovah shall arise upon thee, and His glory shall be seen upon thee " (Isa. 60. 1, 2). As the tiny raindrop, when exposed to the sun, may refract its rays and display all the beautiful colours of the rainbow, so we, too, though very opaque in ourselves, yet in the presence of the Sun of Righteousness may become beautiful in His beauty and glorious in His glory.

"We all with unveiled face beholding as in a mirror, the glory of the Lord, are changed into the same image from glory to glory; even as from the Lord the Spirit " (2 Cor. 3. 18).

Moses speaks of Joseph as being separated from his brethren. He was separated from them not only by distance in space, but also morally by his spiritual character. This was specially the case with our Lord Who was

"Holy, guileless, undefiled, separated from sinners, and made higher than the heavens " (Heb. 7. 26).

He mingled with the crowds, and was different from them all in nature and character. He touched the leper but did not contract his leprosy; He ate with the publicans and sinners, but did not descend to their level, He rather raised them to a higher moral and spiritual platform.

Moses concludes his sublime prediction of Joseph by comparing him to a young bullock in its magnificent strength, and to the buffalo and its mighty horns with which his descendants, Ephraim and Manasseh, would conquer the nations from afar. As one instance, this promise was fulfilled to Gideon, a descendant of Joseph, to whom the Heavenly Messenger said: "Go in this thy might and thou shalt save Israel from the hand of Midian " (Judges 6. 14). It was in the divinely imparted promise that Gideon pushed the Midianites from the land of Israel.

According to tradition, on Ephraim's standard was emblazoned the figure of an ox, corresponding to one of the faces of the Cherubim.

Psa. 105. 16-22 forms a Divine commentary on Joseph's history and throws much light upon it, each line gives us a picture of Christ.

"And He called for a famine upon the land;
He brake the whole staff of bread.
He sent a man before them;
Joseph was sold for a servant.
His feet they hurt with fetters;
His soul entered into the iron,
Until the time that his word came to pass, the word of Jehovah refined him.
The king sent and loosed him;
Even the ruler of the peoples, and let him go free.
He made him lord of all his house, and ruler of his substance;
To bind his princes at his pleasure,
And teach his elders wisdom. "

In Heb. 11. 22, Joseph is held up before us as a hero of great faith,

"By faith Joseph, when his end was nigh, made mention of the departure of the children of Israel; and gave commandment concerning his bones" (Heb. 11. 22).

Joseph (representing Ephraim) and Manasseh, as separate tribes, are mentioned among the sealed of Israel in Rev. 7. They also have separate portions in the restored land (Ezek. 48. 4, 5), but in the gates of the new city, where the tribe of Levi is included, they are united under the name of Joseph, and thus make up the number twelve (Ezek. 48. 31, 32).

Thus will the grace of our unchanging God be

displayed in them to the end of time, and in the words of Joshua, Joseph's renowned son, they will have to acknowledge that not one thing hath failed of all the good things the Lord spake concerning them (Josh. 23. 14).

"BLEST of the Lord was Joseph's land
With sacred treasures of the dew and deep ;
Blest by the moon in Nature's hour of sleep,
And by the sun with autumn's golden heap,
    To fill the Reaper's hand.

His was the strength of ancient hills,
The treasure of the pasture and the mine ;
And, crowning all, a blessing more divine,
Clear in that light that made the Bush to shine,
    Leapt his rejoicing rills.

Blest was his portion when beside
The well of Sychar sat the Holy One,
Footsore and weary 'neath a shadeless sun,
Opening to one who sin's career had run
    Salvation's healing tide.

Bald Ebal and fair Gerizim,
Ages have passed but lightly o'er your brow ;
But o'er your wandering tribes hangs even now
The curse that hath avenged the broken vow
    Of faithless Ephraim.

Yet to His record's promise true,
The Man of Sychar cometh once again,
All Gerizim's rich blessings in his train,
To pour on Joseph's land the latter rain,
    And Shiloh's life renew."
                PAULIN.

Benjamin—Son of the Right Hand

" Benjamin shall ravin as a wolf ;
  In the morning he shall devour the prey,
  And at night he shall divide the spoil "

(Gen. 49. 27).

" Of Benjamin, he said,
  The beloved of the Lord shall dwell in safety by Him,
  He covereth him all the day long,
  And He dwelleth between his shoulders "

(Deut. 33. 12).

CHAPTER XV

Benjamin—Son of the Right Hand

Benoni—the son of my sorrow
Benjamin—the son of the right hand.

The Change of Name.

THE story of Benjamin's birth is very pathetic·
While journeying from Bethel to Ephrath,
Rachel, Jacob's beloved wife, was taken ill,
and gave birth to a child; and her midwife, seeing
her greatly distressed in labour, sought to comfort
her, saying: "Fear not, for this is also a son to thee."
The son was born, but the poor mother died in giving
birth to him, so with her last breath she sought to
commemorate her suffering by calling the child
Benoni—"the son of my sorrow." The father,
however, who could not bear to have, in his son's
name, a constant reminder of this distressing occur-
rence and the death of his beloved Rachel, changed
the name to Benjamin—"the son of the right hand,"
expressing by it also the hope that the boy would
be a means of comfort and strength to him. (Gen.
35. 16-19).

Renewed Promises.

Jacob was encouraged to do this, by the fact that
God had just appeared to him and confirmed to him
the change of his own name from Jacob to Israel,
and repeated to him the promise to bless him and make
him fruitful (Gen. 35. 9-12).

Jacob, also, finding himself at Bethel, where God first revealed Himself to him and gave him many precious promises, on his part renewed his allegiance to Jehovah, and reconsecrated the place that his wonderful experiences there must have made very dear to him; now erecting, perhaps, a more suitable or durable pillar and pouring on it a drink-offering and oil (Gen. 35. 14).

This act of worship prepared the Patriarch to endure the heavy trials that came upon him soon after, and inspired him with fresh fortitude and hope. The birth of another son, the twelfth, who was the only one of all his children born in the promised land, became to him a pledge and earnest that all the gracious promises of God would be fulfilled to him and to his descendants.

Is it not thus with us also? As we get a vision of our Covenant-keeping God in His greatness and goodness, and recall the precious promises He has given us in His Word, we become fortified to endure the troubles of life and take a more hopeful outlook on the days to come, trusting Him Who has said: "I will never leave thee nor forsake thee." The sunshine of His presence dispels the dark clouds around us, and His benignant promises bring to us happy expectations for future days.

   "Benjamin shall ravin as a wolf,
     In the morning he shall devour the prey,
     And at night he shall divide the spoil" (Gen. 49. 27).

The Tribal Characteristic.

This is an accurate description of the tribe, which possessed a courageous and warlike character, as it was exhibited by them when bravely, though wrongly, they defied the combined forces of all the other tribes of Israel in their reckless defence of the wicked men of Gibeah, and in the first two days actually slew 40,000 men of Israel, while their own army only numbered 26,700 men, and the other tribes numbered 400,000. Seven hundred of these Benjamites were left-handed; and "every one of them could sling stones at an hairbreadth and not miss" (Judges 20. 16). The Benjamites are frequently spoken of as skilled archers (1 Chron. 8. 40; 2 Chron. 14. 8). After the great battle against Sisera, Deborah makes honourable mention of that tribe (Judges 5. 14).

Ehud.

The same trait of character was shown by men of Benjamin, such as Ehud, the left-handed warrior-judge, who, having made for himself a sword with two edges for the purpose, single-handed attacked and slew Eglon, the stout-hearted king of Moab, Israel's oppressor, and thus delivered his people.

Saul and Jonathan.

Saul, Israel's first king, was also a Benjamite of Gibeah. He, with wolf-like daring, fought and subdued Israel's enemies.

His son, Jonathan, displayed remarkable courage when he smote the Philistine garrison at Geba, and again at Michmash. In the latter place he climbed a steep crag, with only his armour-bearer as fellow-warrior, in order to attack a numerous foe, and by gaining a complete victory he re-animated the dis-spirited Israelites and turned defeat into victory.

Right at the end of his career we see him engaged in desperate conflict on the mountains of Gilboa, fighting heroically till slain by the enemy. Well did David lament him:

"From the blood of the slain,
From the fat of the mighty,
The bow of Jonathan turned not back,
And the sword of Saul returned not empty . . .
How are the mighty fallen in the midst of the
battle,
Jonathan is slain on the high places . . .
How are the mighty fallen,
And the weapons of war perished!" (2 Sam. 1.
22, 25, 27).

A Retrograde Step.

In the days of Saul, the small tribe of Benjamin
played an important role, and retained their wolf-
like character.

Saul was the *people's* choice. Originally God
formed Israel into a Theocracy; Himself being their
King, while they were intended to be a kingdom of
priests, an holy nation *"above all peoples"* in praise,
in name, and in honour (Exodus 19. 6; Deut. 26.
18, 19); but when they appointed unto themselves an
earthly king they became, as they rightly expressed
it, *"like all the nations"* (1 Sam. 8. 19, 20); it was a
great step downward.

We are not surprised that some of the tribe were
influenced by David and became dissatisfied with
Saul.

Amongst David's "mighty men, his helpers in
war," that came to him in Ziklag, first on the list
are mentioned Saul's brethren of Benjamin, who were
armed with bows; ambidexters, who "could use both
the right hand and the left in slinging stones, and in
shooting arrows from the bow." It is striking that
the two chief men amongst them were Ahiezer and
Joash, the sons of Shemaah of Gibeah, Saul's native
city (1 Chron. 12. 1-3).

A Foreshadowing of the Future.

Have we not, in this history, an adumbration of what will take place at the return of our Lord when, recognising our Lord as Messiah and Saviour, the Jewish people will leave their leaders who have led them astray, and will rally round the standard of Christ? Also many of the nations, enlightened by the Spirit of God, will recognise the deception of the Antichrist and will come to the Lord Jesus, and, acknowledging His moral excellence and rightful authority as King, will submit themselves to Him. In the words of the Psalmist they will confess,

"All the gods of the nations are idols,
But Jehovah made the heavens . . .
Give unto Jehovah, O ye kindreds of the peoples,
Give unto Jehovah glory and strength . . .
O worship Jehovah in the beauty of holiness,
Fear before Him all the earth,
Say among the nations, Jehovah reigneth;
The world also shall be established that it shall not be moved;
He shall judge the peoples righteously."
(Psa. 96. 7, 9, 10).

Heroes of the Exile.

We must not forget Mordecai and Esther, Benjamites who gave credit to that tribe during the Exile, and who, by their fidelity to God and love for their people, brought such a remarkable deliverance to them.

Mordecai dared to resist the proud Haman, and did not bow to him in spite of the king's command that all should do so; and Esther had the courage to approach Ahasuerus uninvited, a thing which no one was allowed to do on penalty of death unless the king held out the golden sceptre.

The inspired writer thought it right to give us their tribal descent (Esther 2. 5-7), from which we learn that they were Benjamites.

A Courageous Apostle.

Saul of Tarsus, the great Apostle of the Gentiles, was also "of the stock of Israel, of the tribe of Benjamin" (Rom. 11. 1; Phil. 3. 5). Before his conversion he persecuted the Jewish believers with the wolf-like ferocity that was characteristic of his tribe, "Making havoc of the Church," and "breathing out threatenings and slaughter against the disciples of the Lord" (Acts 8. 3, and 9. 1). But after his conversion he spread the truth of the Gospel with an earnest determination beyond any of his fellow-apostles, though it meant great privation and suffering to him. Thus, in persecuting the Church he may be likened to a wolf devouring the prey, and in the wonderful blessing that followed, his ministry may be described as dividing the spoil.

We, too, need to have boldness in our service for Christ, and not to be daunted by difficulties and persecution, that we also may enjoy the spoils of victory. Truly,
"They that sow in tears shall reap in joy—He that goeth forth and weepeth, bearing seed for scattering, shall surely come again with rejoicing, bearing his sheaves with him" (Psa. 126. 5, 6).

God's Dwelling Place in Benjamin.

While Jacob in his blessing, speaks of Benjamin as a people, Moses takes into his prediction the portion of land allotted to them, as he also does to Joseph and some of the other tribes.

Benjamin's territory was small, but it occupied an important position between the two great tribes.

Judah on the south, and Ephraim on the north. It included Mizpeh, which at one time formed a great centre in the land; Gibeon, where was for some time the Tabernacle with its altar (1 Chron. 21. 29; 2 Chron. 1. 3); Bethel—the house of God, where Jehovah appeared twice to Jacob, though, alas! Jeroboam afterwards established a corrupt form of worship in that place; and Mount Moriah, on which Solomon built the Temple (2 Chron. 3. 1).

It is highly probable that Deut. 33. 12 refers to this prophetically, Jehovah covering him and dwelling between his shoulders, *i.e.*, having His dwelling place amongst them. There is a beautiful parallel to this in Isa. 4. 5,

> "And Jehovah will create over the whole habitation of Mount Zion, and over her assemblies, a cloud and smoke by day, and the shining of a flaming fire by night, for over all the glory shall be a covering. "

This also has reference to the Temple Area; the word *chupah*, translated "covering" ("defence" in the Authorised Version) is only found three times in the Bible, and comes from the root verb *chaphaph*, "to cover, " used in Deut. 33. 12, and nowhere else. The connection between these two passages is, therefore, fairly evident.

The Typical Aspect of the Name.

The name Benjamin calls to our mind the Lord Jesus, the Son of God's right hand. From this standpoint the words of Rachel, when she gave birth to Joseph, are significant. We are told, "She called his name Joseph, saying, Jehovah shall add to me another son" (Gen. 30. 24).

As we have already seen, Joseph, in many ways foreshadowed the Lord Jesus, so also by his very name he was an earnest that God would add *another Son*.

Primarily, of course, this was fulfilled when his younger brother Benjamin was born, but typically, it was also true of the Other Son that God promised throughout the Scripture, commencing with Eve, the first mother of mankind.   For He is the seed of the woman (Gen. 3. 15), the seed of Abraham (Gen. 22. 28), the seed of Isaac (Gen. 26. 4), the seed of Jacob (Gen. 28. 14), the descendant of Judah (Gen. 49. 10), the Son of David—the other Benjamin—the Son of God's right hand.

The Significance of the Double Name.

Benoni—the son of my sorrow—surely sets forth Christ in His suffering, as "a Man of sorrows and acquainted with grief" (Isa. 53. 3).   But Benjamin speaks to us of Him Who declared concerning Himself: "Hereafter shall ye see the Son of Man sitting on the right hand of power, and coming in the clouds of Heaven" (Matt. 26. 64).   Indeed, His apparent defeat on the Cross was turned into the greatest spiritual victory the world has ever witnessed.

The prophet predicts of Him:
"He shall see of the travail of His soul and shall be satisfied" (Isa. 53. 11).
and the apostle assures us:
"For the joy that was set before Him (He) endured the Cross, despising the shame, and is set down at the right hand of the· throne of God" (Heb. 12. 2).

Messiah's Vicarious Suffering.

There is a striking verse which reads:
"Let Thy hand be upon the man of Thy right hand, upon the Son of man Whom Thou madest strong for Thyself" (Psa. 80. 17).

Who is this Man at God's right hand, this Son of Man made strong for Himself?

Primarily it may be a play on the name of Benjamin (see verse 2), the stock planted by God's right hand and made strong to be His witness (verse 15), but in a deeper sense it is applicable to Christ, the Man at God's right hand, the Son of Man made strong to bring into effect God's wonderful purpose for the salvation of the human race.

The meaning of the expression, "Let Thy hand be upon the man," may be gathered from such verses as Job 19. 21:

"Have pity upon me, have pity upon me, O ye my friends, for the hand of God hath touched me."

It is the hand of chastisement. Again David prayed when the plague was raging against Israel:

"Let Thy hand be against me and against my father's house" (2 Sam. 24. 17).

He was willing to bear the punishment instead of his people; so here (Psa. 80. 17) the Psalmist prays that God's hand of chastisement should be upon the Greater David Who was, indeed, "wounded for our transgressions, and bruised for our iniquities, the chastisement bringing us peace was upon Him, and with His stripes we are healed" (Isa. 53. 5).

In order that Israel should enjoy the sunshine of God's face (vv. 3, 7, 19) their sin had to be dealt with, so the Psalmist pleads that the punishment of their sin should be put upon the Man at God's right hand, the Son of Man Who was made strong for that purpose.

Not Two Messiahs.

In order to explain the prophecies concerning Messiah's suffering, the Rabbis invented a legend that there should be two Messiahs, one, the Son of

Joseph, who was to suffer and die; and another the Son of David, who was to be victorious and reign. As we know, this idea of two Messiahs is absolutely foreign to the Bible, which only speaks of one Messiah, Who must first suffer and die, and then come back in power and glory, to reign in peace and righteousness. Benoni was the same person as Benjamin.

Thus it was that the Heavenly Messengers assured the apostles as they stood looking steadfastly towards Heaven where the Lord ascended.

> *"This same Jesus*, Who is taken up from you into Heaven, shall so come in like manner as ye have seen Him go into Heaven" (Acts 1. 10, 11).

This same Jesus, Who died on the Cross to atone for our sin is to "appear the second time apart from sin unto salvation" (Heb. 9. 28).

All through this dispensation the Lord Jesus is seated at God's right hand, till His enemies are made His footstool (Matt. 22. 44; Acts 2. 34; Heb. 1. 13), and then, as the Mighty Conqueror He will come forth from the opened Heaven crowned with many diadems. On His side and on His garment shall be a name written, KING OF KINGS AND LORD OF LORDS. Sighs and tears will give way to shouts of joy and triumph. Benoni will henceforth be known as Benjamin.

Words of Spiritual Import.

Taking the words of Moses (Deut. 33. 12) as applying also to Christ, we find in them a great truth. "The beloved of the Lord shall dwell in safety by Him." This agrees with the meaning of the name Benjamin; indeed, it is an explanation of it. Our Lord, sitting at the right hand of the Father, dwells in safety by Him.

After the suffering the Lord Jesus endured on earth,

the agonies of Gethsemane, and the tortures of Calvary, He was raised from the dead, and He ascended to the Father beyond the insults and molestations of men, according to His promise, "I will set Him in safety from him that puffeth at Him" (oppresseth Him, Gesenius, Psa. 12. 5).

As foreshadowing the Messiah, Benjamin is called "the Beloved of Jehovah," a term very appropriate to Christ. Has not God Himself declared of Him, "This is My beloved Son, in Whom I am well pleased"?

The remainder of the verse also expresses the close and intimate relationship there was between the Lord Jesus and the Father.

"Jehovah shall cover Him all the day long (continuously),
And He shall dwell between His shoulders."

We cannot imagine a time when Christ did not enjoy His Father's presence and companionship. The prophet foresaw it when he wrote:

"There shall come forth a shoot out of the stem of Jesse,
And a branch out of his roots shall bear fruit,
And upon Him shall rest the Spirit of Jehovah,
The Spirit of wisdom and understanding,
The Spirit of counsel and might,
The Spirit of knowledge and fear of Jehovah"
(Isa. 11. 1, 2).

That is, the Spirit of God in His sevenfold fulness shall rest on the Messiah.

Again the prophet exclaims in the Name of God:

"Behold My Servant Whom I uphold,
Mine Elect in Whom My soul delighteth,
I have put My Spirit upon Him,
He shall bring forth judgment to the nations"
(Isa. 42. 1).

Then, as in response to this, Messiah says:
"The Spirit of Jehovah is upon Me,
Because Jehovah hath anointed Me to preach
good tidings to the meek,
He hath sent Me to bind up the broken-hearted,
And the opening of the prison to them that are
bound" (Isa. 61. 1).

In fulfilment of this we read that out of the opened
Heaven the Spirit of God descended upon Christ like
a dove, and a voice declared, "This is My beloved
Son in Whom I am well pleased" (Matt. 3. 16, 17).

"The beloved of the Lord shall dwell in safety by
Him," contains also a precious promise to all who
dwell in the secret place of the Most High and abide
under the shadow of the Almighty.

"He will cover thee with His pinions,
And under His wings shalt thou take refuge"
(Psa. 91. 1, 2, 4).

It is more important to be loved of the Lord than of
Jacob.

Conclusion

Marks of Inspiration.

The remarkable harmony there is between Jacob and Moses in these prophetic utterances, and the wonderful accuracy with which they were fulfilled in the history of Israel, clearly indicate their Divine origin. To such an extent is this true that some of the modern critics declared them to be a *vaticinium post eventum,* a professed "prophecy after the event."

No human sagacity could, of course, predict a series of events true to history like these, but the writers were inspired by Him Who, by His infinite wisdom, knows the end from the beginning, and by His infinite power controls all the occurrences of the world, ruling and overruling everything according to His will.

Jacob was conscious that he was uttering great prophecies when

"He called unto his sons, and said, Gather yourselves together that I may tell you that which shall befall you *in the latter days.*"

Weak in body, but strong in spirit, the dying Patriarch ended his earthly career in witnessing for God, and blessing his sons, even as he himself received his father's benediction. Indeed, his prophecy was in harmony with the blessings of Abraham and Isaac.

His great faith was exhibited by his statement to Joseph:

"Behold I die; but God will be with you and bring you again unto the land of your fathers" (Gen. 48. 21).

Moses also ended up his earthly course with the prophetic benediction of his people. The wonderful vision given him of God's greatness and goodness in His dealings with Israel, caused him to exclaim:

"There is none like unto the God of Jeshurun,
Who rideth upon the Heavens for thy help,
And in His excellency on the skies" (Deut. 33. 26).

Jeshurun is a name for Israel, and means "the upright," not because they were without fault or sin, but (a) because it was what they were meant to be in the purpose of their calling, and (b) because God, in His forgiving love put the righteousness of His Beloved Son upon them.

"He hath not beheld iniquity in Jacob, neither hath He seen perverseness in Israel" (Num. 23. 21).

It is thus in grace and love that God deals with His children. We, too, experience the blessedness of "the man whose transgression is forgiven, whose sin is covered, and unto whom Jehovah imputeth not iniquity" (Psa. 32. 2).

Moses' final word is one of congratulation to Israel on their relationship with Jehovah, and well may he cry out:

"Happy art thou, O Israel,
Who is like unto thee, a people saved by Jehovah,
The shield of thy help,
And the sword of thy excellency" (Deut. 33. 29).

Israel, like ourselves, has no reason for boasting of their goodness or their greatness, but every reason for glorying in their God.

These verses remind us of the striking passage with which Micah finishes his great prophecy:

"Who is a God like unto Thee, that pardoneth iniquity, and passeth by the transgression of the remnant of His heritage? He retaineth not His anger for ever, because He delighteth in mercy.

He will turn again, He will have compassion upon us; He will subdue our iniquities: and Thou wilt cast all their sins into the depths of the sea. Thou wilt perform the truth to Jacob, and the mercy to Abraham, which Thou hast sworn unto our fathers from the days of old" (Micah 7. 18-20).

The Tribes

PROCLAIM to earth's remotest bound—the hour for which
    ye sigh ;
The hour that Israel waits for—Redemption draweth nigh !
The Woman's Seed—the Star of Jacob—Judah's royal Lion,
Is Coming with His myriad host to reign on ancient Zion !
Is Coming to Mount Olivet to plant His footsteps there,
Whence long ago His chariot-cloud clove the blue morning air.

Simeon shall sing " The Lord hath heard " ; behold, behold
    the Man !
"My God hath judged me," shall sound from all the tents
    of Dan.
From Judah's hills shall cleave the sky the Hallel note of
    " praise."
The " Son of Sorrow " catch the strain, and bless the day of
    days.
Of " fruitfulness " and joy restored shall Ephraim's glory ring,
" Forgetfulness " of grief shall make Manasseh's woodlands
    ring.

The plain of Jezreel shall bloom like rod of ancient Aaron,
When meets the lily of the vale the bridegroom Rose of
    Sharon.
Strong Issachar shall joy to see the long-expected " Hire,"
And Zebulun's fair " dwelling " ring with voice of gladsome
    choir ;
Asher in " happiness " shall haste to meet the righteous One,
And Naphtali, the " Hind let loose," shall leap from Lebanon.

Old Jordan bound rejoicingly with all thy glorious rills,
For soon the light of ancient days shall shine along the hills ;
Thy banks shall wear a brighter bloom, and Gilead's tree
    of balm
Shall waft commingling odours with the cedar and the palm ;
When Reuben shall his King behold—a Son of Judah's line,
And Gad shall lead his bannered " Troop " to hail the Man
    Divine."   G. PAULIN.